WRITING
— *for* —
BUSINESS

WRITING
— for —
BUSINESS

Case Exercises in Effective Business Writing

DENNIS SIGNOROVITCH

WRITING FOR BUSINESS
CASE EXERCISES IN EFFECTIVE BUSINESS WRITING

iUniverse books may be ordered through booksellers or by contacting:

iUniverse
1663 Liberty Drive
Bloomington, IN 47403
www.iuniverse.com
844-349-9409

Because of the dynamic nature of the Internet, any web addresses or links contained in this book may have changed since publication and may no longer be valid. The views expressed in this work are solely those of the author and do not necessarily reflect the views of the publisher, and the publisher hereby disclaims any responsibility for them.

Any people depicted in stock imagery provided by Getty Images are models, and such images are being used for illustrative purposes only. Certain stock imagery © Getty Images.

ISBN: 978-1-6632-1664-9 (sc)
ISBN: 978-1-6632-1665-6 (e)

Library of Congress Control Number: 2021905696

Print information available on the last page.

iUniverse rev. date: 06/15/2021

To the memory of Susan

Writing is thinking. To write well is to think clearly.
That's why it's so hard.

—David McCullough

If you can't explain what you're doing in plain English,
you're probably doing something wrong.

—Alfred E. Kahn

CONTENTS

PREFACE

To Students

An unexpected satisfaction I discovered as a college instructor, after a long career in business, was the occasional communication from former students updating me on their careers. I soon noticed that a number of these emails from young professionals two or three or more years out of college were well written. At first, I assumed that my efforts to improve their writing had—at long last and in the fullness of time—paid off.

But modesty quickly got the upper hand, and I came to accept, however reluctantly, that my correspondents were simply more experienced. They'd had more occasions to do writing relevant to their jobs and careers paths. My earlier attempts to grind away at sentence length, word choice, passive construction, proofreading, and all the other precepts of acceptable writing had sunk in or faded away, but in either case, these were now subordinated to the professional need to write clearly. Their emails were less the result of instruction than of experience.

This small book is rooted in the simple, perhaps obvious, insight that you learn to write well through practice. The cases included here will give you a head start on the process of regular business writing. The introduction and first chapter provide advice on how to analyze the cases and some basic guidelines and guardrails to help in writing. Make yourself familiar with this material. But the real value will be found in the cases and the accompanying writing tasks.

None of the assignments demand the thorough research and lengthy assessment that goes into a college term paper. That's not the intent. Instead, they involve writing a cover note encouraging the sales team, a message to employees, a letter to the board of directors, or an invitation to a company's suppliers. These are the kind of writing tasks you're most likely to encounter in business.

Even in a communications environment that often seems to rely on little more than terse, punctuation-free messages sent on mobile devices, the ability to write well matters. Employers look for writing skills in job prospects *and* their current staff members too. It will increase your value as an employee and, in time, contribute to your success.

To Instructors

This compilation of writing exercises is aimed directly at your undergraduate business students. The cases present a variety of writing tasks found in the business world rather than typical college writing assignments. They can supplement the assigned textbooks across much of the business curriculum. They may prove especially useful in courses offered to third- and fourth-year students, including courses on management principles, organizational behavior, marketing, and management communications.

The cases lend themselves to substantive classroom discussion. In some respects, these class sessions can simulate meetings that occur in an organization before action is taken. Consider using the worksheet in the first chapter to structure the critical thinking that must precede writing. Encourage students to probe beneath the surface of each case to identify issues that should inform the writing in matters such as tone, urgency, or unstated motivations of the individuals involved. What facts and details should be used? In what order should they be arranged to make the message clear and compelling? Which can be ignored? Make it clear to your students that in their roles as the writers in each case, the messages they produce will reflect on them just as they would if they were junior staff members in an actual business.

Also, discourage students from trying to find the "right" answer to each case. Effective business writing is clear and persuasive, not categorically right or wrong. Some students might find this unsettling; how could they not after so many years spent in classrooms? Help them understand that the business world does not come with a textbook that has the correct answers conveniently found in the back. The cases also can be used for oral presentations—not magic-lantern slideshows that risk anesthetizing the listener but tightly structured in-class briefings that synthesize the key points of a student's written reports combined with a chance to hone students' skills at speaking in business meetings.

Regardless of how you present the cases, keep them coming over the course of the semester. They are intended for a quick turnaround, perhaps a weekend or a few days. The learning is linked with the frequency of the assignments.

The checklist in the first chapter provides a useful way to measure and track the success of each writing submission. You can use the scoring scale to evaluate students' work. Alternatively, have students score their work first and then offer your score on each element of the checklist. The difference between the two scores can generate a rewarding dialogue about the effectiveness of the student's writing. But no matter how you elect to use the cases and worksheets, the fundamental premise of *Writing for Business* remains that student writing improves through regular practice.

Finally, the cases are intended to be realistic, but some of the layers of complexity in an actual business setting have been pared back to improve comprehension and make the writing tasks more manageable for students. If, in the process of doing so, the cases have lost a measure of realism, it was a deliberate decision on my part.

ACKNOWLEDGMENTS

The students who took up the challenge of effective business writing over the years inspired me to write this casebook. It's my hope that the undergraduates who follow in their footsteps will benefit from what I have learned from them.

A stalwart group of friends and colleagues, past and present, generously gave their time to read the cases. At different times and places, several of them were with me on the corporate communications front lines where a good deal of writing was done. All of the following contributed insights and suggestions that inform the case studies: Mike Ascolese, Lauren Astor, Howard Blumberg, Dan Burnham, Dr. Michael French, Terrence "Mick" Grasmick, Ron Iori, Dr. David Leese, Joe Leonard, Ernie Linneman, Bill Reavis, Andy Tannen, Michael Timmermann, and Don Wilt. My thanks to each of them. I also want to express my gratitude to Chantal Randolph at Mount St. Mary's for her cheerful and always dependable efforts to keep my various projects running smoothly. She unfailingly laughs at my lame jokes too.

I knew the tables would turn eventually and that Sarah Signorovitch and James Signorovitch would get a chance to edit my writing. They did so, at times, in excruciating detail, but with a much-appreciated level of tact. It's been my good fortune to have such devoted children.

My loving wife, Janet Hindler, never let her feelings impinge on her role as my exacting senior editor. Despite her own career commitments, she read each case with the care and thoroughness she brings to everything she does. Her advice improved this book, just as she has made every aspect of my life better.

Los Angeles, CA
January, 2021

INTRODUCTION

"**S**trong communication skills required." The phrase appears so frequently in job postings that eager applicants might see it as little more than wallpaper in a job listing. They shouldn't. Communication—and its foundational skill, effective writing—is a vital component of most careers. A recent survey by the National Association of Colleges and Employers found that written communication ranked among the top attributes employers want in an applicant.[1] Yet the decline in writing ability among job prospects remains a source of continuing frustration for many hiring managers.

Writing skill also is listed frequently by university and college faculty as an essential outcome of an undergraduate education. Paradoxically, some college courses reportedly limit the amount of writing required. In their book *Academically Adrift*, Richard Arum and Josipa Roksa[2] found that 50 percent of the undergraduate students they surveyed said they did not have a single course requiring at least twenty pages of writing in their previous semester. Yet there are no shortcuts along the way to effective business writing. It only improves with regular practice. This book is intended as a step in that direction.

---

[1] National Association of Colleges and Employers, "Key Attributes Employers Want to See on Students' Resumes," NACEweb.org, January 13, 2020.

[2] Richard Arum and Josipa Roksa, *Academically Adrift: Limited Learning on College Campuses* (Chicago: University of Chicago Press, 2011). The book's conclusions were questioned by some academics for relying on limited data. In 2018, Arum announced a new and more ambitious study involving experts from over a dozen institutions and funding from the Andrew W. Mellon Foundation.

Understanding the Cases

The cases offer you an opportunity to practice your writing skills in settings you might encounter in your career. They are written in the second person singular (i.e., *you*) in order to situate you in the case not as an outside observer but as someone in the fray who must act on the assignment.

There are no study points or prompts appended to the cases. Nor are there specific word counts for each assignment.[3] As helpful as these devices can be in a classroom, they are not naturally occurring phenomena in the business world. Quite often in business, an issue, an opportunity, or a challenge is identified. It's discussed and analyzed, a decision is made, and then a task is assigned without much attention to communications formalities. The cases attempt to create that just-get-it-done immediacy.

Each case presents a situation that actually occurs in businesses large and small: the need to revise a business model that no longer works well, a company facing sagging customer demand, businesses that encounter difficulties when they overreach or struggle in shifting markets, the compelling need to make sure a new product launch is successful or a new ERP system is well received in the company, changing relationships with suppliers and vendors, irate customers, workforce diversity challenges, and the always present need to manage your career.

Ideally, the issue in each case should be discussed during a class meeting or at a breakout session, just as it would in an actual business setting. Use that opportunity to ask questions, to clear up uncertainties about the facts, and to resolve any apparent ambiguities. Getting everything straight in your mind builds the foundation for effective business writing.

The assignments demand individual effort rather than the team-based work frequently stressed in business courses. However important

---

[3] I once heard of a young staffer who asked a manager how many words an assignment should be. "Give it what it's worth," she was told in reply.

learning to function in groups may be, the ability to write well is not a skill that can be delegated to a team. It requires individual, perhaps even solitary, effort. A team can too easily assign the written work product to the best writer in the group, leaving every other team member off the hook. This exercise book expects you to build and strengthen your writing ability, just like every other student.

There are two fundamental parts of an effective response to each case. The first includes the basics of written business communications: correct grammar, accurate spelling, and accessible, concise sentence structure. In short, have you made yourself clear? The second involves an element of judgment and discretion in how you write the assignment. What facts do you use in developing the message? In what order are they used? Are there details in the case that can be ignored entirely? Successful business writing must address both parts. A case that seems straightforward at first glance might require more thoughtful consideration.

Finally, those of you studying communications as a gateway to jobs in public relations or marketing communications will benefit from the writing assignments, but the cases are designed to challenge those pursuing careers in accounting, human resources, marketing, sales, and operations too. Perhaps you expect, or hope, that your career goals will not make demands on your writing ability. But experience shows that they will. These demands will present themselves when they're least expected, and they might well occur early in your career.

See these unanticipated writing tasks as opportunities, not undesirable chores. They are an occasion to grow, even if they force you out of your comfort zone. "Growth and comfort do not coexist,"[4] Virginia Rometty, the former IBM chair and CEO, has said.

There's no avoiding the fact that writing well is a challenge. "Writing is hard, even for authors who do it all the time," says Roger Angell, a celebrated writer at *The New Yorker*. "Less frequent practitioners—the

---

[4] Andrew Nusca, "IBM's Rometty: Growth and Comfort Don't Co-Exist," *Fortune*, October 7, 2014. https://fortune.com/2014/10/7/ibms-rometty-growth-and-comfort-dont-coexist/

job applicant; the business executive ... often get stuck in an awkward passage or find a muddle on their screens, and then blame themselves. What should be easy and flowing looks tangled or feeble or overblown— not what was meant at all."[5]

The Enduring Value of Good Writing

Learning to write is worth the effort. Strong writing ability is a competitive advantage. It can strengthen your marketability at every point in your career. Confidence in your writing may also carry over into other aspects of your professional life. Effective writing requires a firm grasp of the facts in a given situation; as such, it can reinforce your self-assurance as a manager.

Many executives and business leaders are good writers. While not in a literary sense (I never encountered an incipient F. Scott Fitzgerald during my years in the corporate world), there are executives who demonstrate a facility for clear and persuasive writing. Usually they value good writing for utilitarian reasons. Jeff Bezos famously insists on starting meetings with all participants reading each other's six-page memos on the issue under consideration. It's not possible to write six pages of complete sentences in narrative form without clear thinking, he contends.

In contrast to those memos, slide presentations replete with two- or three-word bullet points may easily remain vague and loosely reasoned. Or, as General James Mattis observed succinctly, "PowerPoint makes us stupid."[6] Andrew Grove, the longtime leader of Intel, viewed writing as a means of self-discipline that forces more precision and clarity into the thought process. And Warren Buffett, the legendary investor and CEO of Berkshire Hathaway, virtually defined the significance of clear writing in business when asked why the company's annual report didn't

---

[5] Roger Angell, *This Old Man, All in Pieces* (New York: Doubleday, 2015), 18.

[6] Elizabeth Bumiller, "We Have Met the Enemy and He is PowerPoint," *New York Times*, April 26, 2010. http://www.nytimes.com/2010/04/27/world/27powerpoint.html?hp.

include glossy photographs: "There are no pictures that would aid in understanding Berkshire, but 10,000 words will—if they are carefully chosen."[7]

In my experience with corporate leaders who wrote well, their writing skill stemmed from their ability to clearly analyze a business situation coupled with their reading of history, biography, or fiction in addition to business articles and books. If one would attempt to locate the wellspring of effective writing skills at the C-suite level, these might be an excellent starting point: analytical ability and wide reading interests.

It's More Than a Toolkit

The first chapter details a number of tools, tips, and examples that can assist you in writing clearly and effectively. They are important, but don't confuse effective writing with a set of tools. In *The Elements of Style,* William Strunk and E. B. White cite a writer who explained that "Writing is an act of faith, not a trick of grammar."[8] Writing requires a commitment to the truth of what is being written, a desire for clarity, and a sincere attempt to ensure that readers will grasp your message. That's easy to say but, as is often the case, the doing can be a challenge. It demands effort.

The best business writing is rooted in a deep understanding of the issues involved. It's not a matter of word processing. The persuasiveness of what you write will depend on how well you grasp the facts and the circumstances in each case and in all the future writing you may be called upon to do in your career. Keep this in mind as you meet those challenges.

---

[7] L. J. Rittenhouse, *Buffett's Bites: The Essential Investor's Guide to Warren Buffett's Shareholder Letters* (New York: McGraw Hill, 2010), 9.

[8] William Strunk Jr. and E. B. White, *The Elements of Style* (New York: Macmillan, 1959), 70.

1

BECOMING AN
EFFECTIVE WRITER

Tools for Successful Business Writing

What does it mean to be a good writer in a business context? Business writing values clarity, accessibility, and directness. It aims to impart information in an efficient, unambiguous manner. While this might seem obvious and easily achieved, all too often convoluted syntax, passive constructions, and jargon create an unappetizing word salad larded with confusion and uncertainty.

In some instances, there is a deliberate attempt to mislead the reader or divert attention. When Enron's 2000 annual report proclaimed that the company "has metamorphosed from an asset-based pipeline and logistics company to a marketing and logistics company whose biggest assets are its well-established business approach and its innovative people,"[9] it telegraphed the deception that led to the company's collapse. But most flaccid or dull business writing results from carelessness or indifference.

There are any number of manuals and style guides an instructor or a student can consult to learn more about clear writing and accurate

---

[9] Enron Corp., 2000 Annual Report, 5.

grammar. Use them to improve your writing.[10] In addition, there are some basic building blocks of communication with which every business writer should be familiar:

- **Purpose**—At first glance, understanding the purpose of a communication might appear easy, even simple-minded. But think through the intent of what's to be communicated. Is it simply to advise? Or, as is more likely, are those on the receiving end expected to act on the communication? What are you trying to achieve?

- **Audience**—Analyze your audience to identify what they expect, know, or assume. Are they anticipating the communication or will it come out of left field? Will they be open to it? Resistant? Skeptical? Curious? And always keep in mind the indirect audience for all your writing. A supervisor is likely to use written work as one way to measure your overall performance and ability to contribute to the organization's results.

- **Context**—Consider the context in which the communication will occur. Is the business facing new or unexpected challenges? Are there unanticipated competitive threats? Is there a new product category or market that the organization must address? Will your audience have the background details needed to understand the situation? Are *you* familiar with those circumstances too?

- **Message**—Ask yourself what you want the audience to take away from the communication. Business communication usually is intended to result in action. Is your message organized in a way to make that clear? Does your message address what's

---

[10] Strunk and White's *The Elements of Style* remains a steadfast writer's companion. For a more contemporary guide to effective writing, consider Roy Peter Clark, *Writing Tools: 55 Essential Strategies for Every Writer*, 10th ed. (New York: Little, Brown Spark, 2016); Harold Evans, *Do I Make Myself Clear? Why Writing Well Matters* (New York: Little, Brown, 2017); or the erudite Francis-Noel Thomas and Mark Turner, *Clear and Simple as the Truth: Writing Classic Prose*, 2nd ed. (Princeton: Princeton University Press, 2011).

in it for the audience? Does it address their concerns or doubts? And, finally, does it really make the sale or just dump a pile of facts in front of the audience?

- **Media**—Each case in this book assigns a writing task, but, as is true in business, how those work products are delivered will vary. Preparing talking points for a meeting or a webinar will necessarily differ from a detailed report to a board of directors, a message to a company's suppliers, or an email to managers. In some circumstances, you may also want to take the initiative and recommend the medium that seems best in a given situation. Do you call angry customers or email them? Do you send a formal message to the staff right outside the boss's office door or prep the boss with talking points? Regardless of whether your recommendation is accepted, it will show that you're someone who thinks about the communications task, not just a scribe taking dictation. Finally, there are several electronic direct messaging applications available for business communications. They are useful for quick and very informal messages or to share information and files on joint projects. They may be appropriate channels for some communications but your message will have to be short and easy to review. Direct messaging environments don't lend themselves to longer or more detailed communications. For example, it might be suitable for a quick update to peers but not for a question to your supervisor that requires a complicated response. Attune yourself to how the organization uses direct messaging. Don't assume that it can replace any other type of business writing.

Communications courses explore these fundamentals as well as many other facets of business communications: oral presentations, media relations, social media, and others. These are important, but they fall outside the scope of this book. Indeed, a strong case can be made that the practice of good writing—the subject of this book—remains at the heart of business communications. Without it, all else suffers.

Teaching communications skills that emphasize today's technologies can be especially limiting. Technology-based skills may have a short shelf life as the technologies, and even the organizations themselves, evolve. But the ability to write well will endure.

Technique Matters

While each case offers a different challenge and requires a clear understanding of the specific details, there are technical features of good writing that apply in every case:

- Prepare an outline to stay on track and avoid wandering off on tangents. Initially, don't worry about having your thoughts in order; just list the points you intend to cover in your writing project, then proceed to organize them logically.
- Be direct. Establish the need or purpose of your communication early.
- Use a conversational tone. Business writing is usually informal, but keep it professional.
- Make sure that your sentences are sentences (i.e., each must have a subject and a predicate).
- Pay attention to sentence length. As a general rule, if your sentence has more than twenty-five words, rewrite it.
- Stop writing once your sentence has made a point. Overly long sentences are more likely to get you into trouble. They can lead to confusion, raise more questions than they answer, and generally leave readers uncertain about your intent
- Check and then recheck your spelling and grammar. Poor grammar and spelling errors are distracting and reflect badly on you. If possible, have someone read your material. Fresh eyes can be helpful. Or, consider using online editing and grammar-checking software.
- Be alert to overwriting and redundancies:

- o Doubling up: "your *own* values," "his *personal* views"
- o Repetition: "the marginal cost *tool* is a *tool* ..."
- o Unnecessary front-end adverbs: *moreover, furthermore, therefore, consequently, as a result.*

- Lose the jargon. You don't have to *interface* with people if you can just meet with them. You don't have to *drill down* on an issue or pick *low-hanging fruit*, either. These terms may have been fresh once but they've *passed their sell-by date.*

- Use formatting devices to highlight your key points: subheads, boldface, a series with numbers or bullets. These will make your writing accessible and easy to scan. But carefully consider how you use these devices. Don't scatter them indiscriminately across the pages. Think of them as signposts helping readers follow your message and grasp the key points. If everything is emphasized, nothing is important.

- Recognize that business writing is not the same as writing college term papers: cover pages, endnotes, bibliographies, and other accouterments of academic writing are typically out of place in business writing.

- When formatting your business writing, don't expect to have the format stipulated, as it often is in classroom settings. In many instances, a standard memo structure (i.e., *To, From, Subject, Date*) is suitable. A reference guide to basic business writing formats is included in the appendix. You can also ask to see how things are generally formatted in your company. But bear in mind that managers will primarily be interested in the *content* of your work. If the format needs to be adjusted, they'll tell you. And they won't be assigning you a letter grade either.

- Read your work aloud. There's a good chance that you will hear any poor grammar, incoherence, and generally weak writing that needs to be revised. If you don't want to listen to the sound of your voice, consider a text-to-speech software program that will do the reading for you. Some are free.

Effective Business Writing from the Real World

Now that we've reviewed some of the basics building blocks, let's take a close look at several examples of effective business writing to identify takeaways you might use in your work.

Over the years, Warren Buffett's annual letters to Berkshire Hathaway Inc. shareholders have been plumbed by those looking for business insights or investment strategies. These are examples of effective business writing too. We can learn from Buffett's easily understood and candid style, although most of us would do well not to attempt his folksy manner.[11]

His 2007 letter describes the types of businesses he likes and why. Without a showy display of jargon-infused strategy-speak, he provides a clear explanation of his reasoning in terms nearly everyone can understand.

---

[11] Warren E. Buffett, *50 Berkshire Hathaway Letters to Shareholders, 1965–2014*, ed. Max Olson (Mountain View, CA: Explorist, 2015). Excerpts from the 2007 and 2008 letters are used with permission.

Warren Buffett's Letter	Takeaways
Let's take a look at what kind of businesses turn us on ... Charlie [Munger, Vice Chairman, Berkshire Hathaway] and I look for companies that have (a) a business we understand; (b) favorable long-term economics; (c) able and trustworthy management; and, (d) a sensible price tag. We like to buy the whole business or, if management is our partner, at least 80%. When control-type purchases of quality aren't available, though, we are also happy to simply buy small portions of great businesses by way of stock-market purchases. It's better to have a part interest in the Hope Diamond than to own all of a rhinestone.	This is how Buffett's letter introduces a new subject. If you've ever lamented, "I don't know how to start!" pay attention to how he does it. It's direct and to the point: "Let's take a look ..."
A truly great business must have an enduring "moat" that protects excellent returns on invested capital. The dynamics of capitalism guarantee that competitors will repeatedly assault any business "castle" that is earning high returns....	There's no way a reader will miss the specific features of a company that Buffett is looking for. They're spelled out: (a), (b), (c).
Our criterion of "enduring" causes us to rule out companies in industries prone to rapid and continuous change. Though capitalism's "creative destruction" is highly beneficial for society, it precludes investment certainty. A moat that must be continuously rebuilt will eventually be no moat at all.	Buffett explains what is meant by a defensible business without resorting to business jargon (e.g., *high barriers to entry*). Instead, he uses the easily understood example of a moat around a castle.
Additionally, this criterion eliminates the business whose success *depends* on having a great manager. Of course, a terrific CEO is a huge asset for any enterprise, and at Berkshire we have an abundance of these managers. Their abilities have created billions of dollars of value that would never have materialized if typical CEOs had been running their businesses.	

But if a business *requires* a superstar to produce great results, the business itself cannot be deemed great. A medical partnership led by your area's premier brain surgeon may enjoy outsized and growing earnings, but that tells little about its future. The partnership's moat will go when the surgeon goes. You can count, though, on the moat of the Mayo Clinic to endure, even though you can't name its CEO.

Long-term competitive advantage in a stable industry is what we seek in a business. If that comes with rapid growth, great. But even without organic growth, such a business is rewarding. We will simply take the lush earnings of the business and use them to buy similar businesses elsewhere. There's no rule that you have to invest money where you've earned it. Indeed, it's often a mistake to do so: Truly great businesses, earning huge returns on tangible assets, *can't* for any extended period reinvest a large portion of their earnings internally at high rates of return.

He acknowledges the important role of business leaders but makes clear that an organization that *requires* a superstar doesn't meet his definition of *great*. And, he uses a compelling example to make his point. (I really need to look up the name of the Mayo Clinic's CEO!)

These are direct, clearly stated goals: long-term advantage in stable industries. Buffett also underscores the need for managers to stay flexible with their investment plans because even "great businesses" are unlikely to achieve high rates of return over extended periods. Again, it's an easily understood message devoid of jargon.

The next year, as the Great Recession devastated the entire economy, Buffett's letter to the Berkshire shareholders stressed the consistency of the company's goals. In a moment of widespread financial anxiety, his words conveyed a sense of calm. And they exemplify effective business writing.

Warren Buffett's Letter	Takeaways
In good years and bad, Charlie and I simply focus on four goals: (1) maintaining Berkshire's Gibraltar-like financial position, which features huge amounts of excess liquidity, near-term obligations that are modest, and dozens of sources of earning and cash; (2) widening the "moats" around our operating businesses that give them durable competitive advantages: (3) acquiring and developing new and varied streams of earnings; (4) expanding and nurturing the cadre of outstanding operating managers who, over the years, have delivered Berkshire's exceptional results.	This is a fine example of concise, explicit, clearly crafted business writing: • appropriately used formatting devices to enumerate goals • understandable, jargon-free metaphors: *Gibraltar-like*, *moats* • remarkably consistent goals, even during the Great Recession

Another notable example of clear business writing is Jeff Bezos's letter to Amazon shareholders when the company went public in 1997. In a real sense, it's a foundational document that defines the company.[12]

---

[12] https://www.aboutamazon.com/news/company-news/amazons-original-1997-letter-to-shareholders.

Jeff Bezos's Letter

Takeways

It's All About the Long Term We believe that a fundamental measure of our success will be the shareholder value we create over the *long term*. This value will be a direct result of our ability to extend and solidify our current market leadership position. The stronger our market leadership, the more powerful our economic model. Market leadership can translate directly to higher revenue, higher profitability, greater capital velocity, and correspondingly stronger returns on invested capital. Our decisions have consistently reflected this focus. We first measure ourselves in terms of the metrics most indicative of market leadership: customer and revenue growth, the degree to which our customers continue to purchase from us on a repeat basis, and the strength of our brand. We have invested and will continue to invest aggressively to expand and leverage our customer base, brand, and infrastructure as we move to establish an enduring franchise. Because of our emphasis on the long term, we may make decisions and weigh tradeoffs differently than some companies. Accordingly, we want to share with you our fundamental management and decision-making approach so that you, our shareholders, may confirm that it is consistent with your investment philosophy:	The company's focus is right there in the headline and repeated in the first sentence: *long term*. It couldn't be more clear, direct, and unequivocal. The phrase *market leadership* is repeated three times in the first paragraph alone. It is unmissable. Amazon outlines its distinctive business approach directly and emphatically so that its shareholders and prospective investors can understand how the company will be managed.

• We will continue to focus relentlessly on our customers.	These bullet points all stress the company's determination in the repetition of *we will* and also in the continued references to *market leadership* as the essential goal. The message couldn't be clearer to investors or to employees.
• We will continue to make investment decisions in light of long-term market leadership considerations rather than short-term profitability considerations or short-term Wall Street reactions.	
• We will continue to measure our programs and the effectiveness of our investments analytically, to jettison those that do not provide acceptable returns, and to step up our investment in those that work best. We will continue to learn from both our successes and our failures.	The specific elements of the management approach are in rank order, not just randomly listed.
• We will make bold rather than timid investment decisions where we see a sufficient probability of gaining market leadership advantages. Some of these investments will pay off, others will not, and we will have learned another valuable lesson in either case.	
• When forced to choose between optimizing the appearance of our GAAP accounting and maximizing the present value of future cash flows, we'll take the cash flows.	
• We will share our strategic thought processes with you when we make bold choices (to the extent competitive pressures allow), so that you may evaluate for yourselves whether we are making rational long-term leadership investments.	

- We will work hard to spend wisely and maintain a lean culture. We understand the importance of continually reinforcing a cost-conscious culture, particularly in a business incurring net losses.

- We will balance our focus on growth with emphasis in long-term profitability and capital management. At this stage, we choose to prioritize growth because we believe that scale is central to achieving the potential of our business model.

- We will continue to focus on hiring and retaining versatile and talented employees, and continue to weight their compensation to stock options rather than cash. We know our success will be largely affected by our ability to attract and retain a motivated employee base, each of whom must think like, and therefore must actually be, an owner.

We aren't so bold as to claim that the above is the "right" investment philosophy, but it's ours, and we would be remiss if we weren't clear in the approach we have taken and will continue to take.

This is vigorous writing that leaves no doubt as to where the company intends to go. Underscoring the significance of this 1997 letter, it's been reprinted in every Amazon annual report since.

Amazon's entire 1997 letter and Berkshire Hathaway's annual letters are valuable examples of effective business writing. But take the initiative to find other examples of strong business writing. Study them carefully and ask yourself:

- What makes them effective?
- What is it about them that makes the message clear, concise, accessible, and compelling?
- How do they make their key points stand out?
- How you can adopt their techniques to improve your writing?

A Worksheet and a Checklist to Get You Started

Whether you're examining a piece of business writing you found during your general reading, working with a case in this book, or even undertaking a writing task at work, the case analysis worksheet and writing checklist included with this chapter can help structure your thinking and your writing. Consider integrating them into all your drafting and editing activities.

Think of the worksheet as the scaffolding needed to build your writing assignment. It can be modified or expanded as needed for a particular case. Use it to (1) identify the audience; (2) describe and detail the message; (3) list the facts with which you can build and support the message; and, finally, (4) prepare an outline. Then you'll be ready to write.

Use the checklist afterward to review and edit your writing. Ask yourself the questions on the checklist, and be honest with your answers. Simply reading through each item on the list without much thought would be equivalent to cheating at solitaire. Consider using the scoring scale in the right-hand column to evaluate your writing even if your instructor doesn't use it for grading. Additional copies of the worksheet and checklist are included in the appendix.

Bear in mind the essential purpose of the worksheet and checklist. They are not inviolable rituals to be performed during and after a writing assignment. Rather, they are intended to foster a way of thinking about the writing process that, over time, will become second nature to you.

Actively engage others in the ongoing effort to strengthen your writing. When a report or paper is returned in your classes, expect more than just a letter grade. Resist the instinct to just see what grade you received and then never give the assignment another thought. Look for editorial comments that can improve your writing; if there aren't any, seek out the instructor and ask for feedback. If your school provides writing coaches, make an appointment and ask the coach for ways to improve your writing even if you received a good grade. Reach out to your fellow students to read your work before you submit it and offer to do the same for them. Even the very best writers need editors.

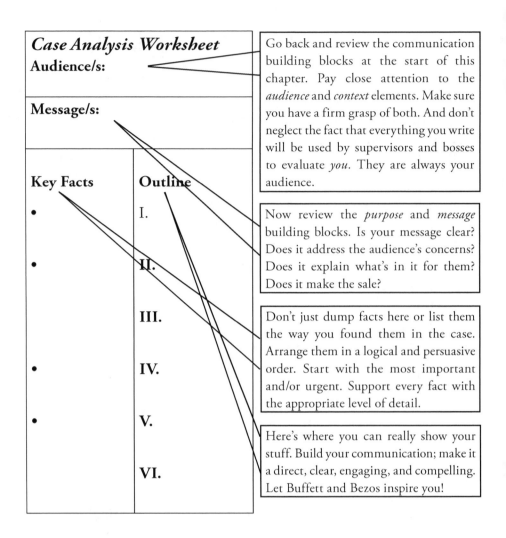

Case Analysis Worksheet

Audience/s:

Go back and review the communication building blocks at the start of this chapter. Pay close attention to the *audience* and *context* elements. Make sure you have a firm grasp of both. And don't neglect the fact that everything you write will be used by supervisors and bosses to evaluate *you*. They are always your audience.

Message/s:

Now review the *purpose* and *message* building blocks. Is your message clear? Does it address the audience's concerns? Does it explain what's in it for them? Does it make the sale?

Key Facts	**Outline**
•	I.
•	II.
	III.
•	IV.
•	V.
	VI.

Don't just dump facts here or list them the way you found them in the case. Arrange them in a logical and persuasive order. Start with the most important and/or urgent. Support every fact with the appropriate level of detail.

Here's where you can really show your stuff. Build your communication; make it a direct, clear, engaging, and compelling. Let Buffett and Bezos inspire you!

Now you can start writing!

Case Writing Checklist

Element	Details	Score Student	Score Instructor
Analysis	Have you delved into the issues in the case or merely summarized the facts?		
Organization	Did you start with an outline and make certain that your writing reflects logical, orderly thinking?		
Diction	Are your word choices exact and appropriate? Have you used phrases and words that are compelling and persuasive?		
Clarity	Have you expressed your ideas and recommendations in a simple, clear, and accessible way?		
Editing	Have you proofread and spellchecked your writing? Have you read it aloud to check for tense agreement, run-on sentences, and fragments? Are the sentences too long or awkward? Is the punctuation correct?		
Conclusion	Do you offer an appropriate summary based on the purpose of the writing assignment (e.g., next steps, timelines, encouragement, a projection of confidence)?		

Scoring Scale

Not Effective	Somewhat Effective	Effective

1.0	1.5	2.0	2.5	3.0

2

CHANGE FOR THE BETTER

*Explaining a New Sales Approach
to the Finance and Sales Teams*

"Our margins are getting killed—not squeezed, killed!"
Greg Allen, always a voluble person, is in rare form this morning. "Customers walk into our stores, and they've already been on the internet and have a fixed price in mind that they're willing to pay. Plus, the carmakers are cutting our dealer percentages on new car sales. We're jammed from both sides!"

Greg is sitting behind the desk in his sports-memorabilia-filled office while staff members perch on every available chair, the leather sofa, and the sofa's armrest. The meeting had been called almost spontaneously, as is Greg's usual style. "We gotta rethink the way we do business," he continues.

Greg is president and CEO of Santa Monica Motors Group, a large automotive dealership organization in Southern California. The group includes several dealerships in the Los Angeles area selling a range of imported vehicles. You started there a few years ago in the group's small marketing and advertising department at the Torrance headquarters and are now the assistant advertising manager reporting to ad manager Bob Valentine. The two of you, along with recently hired marketing associate Alyssa Turner, sales VP Ken Colston, finance VP

Mike Leonard, and a couple of his finance staffers, are there to listen as Greg outlines the company's predicament.

He's not wrong about the squeeze. The average profit margin earned on new-vehicle sales was 1.2 percent last year, down from 2.1 percent when you started with the company. That's left the Santa Monica Motors stores to rely increasingly on add-on products that can add to the final price of the vehicle, like insurance for dings and scratches; coverage for wheel and tire damage; and extended warranties. Across all the group's stores, the dollar value of these added services has reached an average of $1,800, up from $1,400 five years ago.

The other important revenue source has been vehicle loan financing. Although customers can arrange financing on their own, about 85 percent of Santa Monica Motors customers get their loans through the dealerships, with revenues of anywhere from a few hundred to thousands of dollars, depending on the size of the loan.

Customers are complaining about the finance-office experience.

"The value of the add-ons is more important than ever," Greg says. "It makes all the difference in the world when it comes down to running a successful business. But it's beginning to look like we need to rethink how we go about it."

Like most other dealerships, Santa Monica Motors has relied on the finance office to drive that add-on revenue. Once customers select a car or truck and settle on a price, they are sent to the finance office, where they arrange their vehicle financing and are offered the whole range of extras. In fact, *offered* isn't exactly the right term. The finance managers often pressure customers to sign up for the warranties and other add-ons. The salespeople in the showrooms make bad jokes about the finance-office gauntlet that every customer has to run before buying a car.

Make sure the finance people don't take it the wrong way.

"Your guys are doing a good job with the add-on sales, Mike, but I'm wondering if the finance office is the best place for it," Greg continues.

"From the feedback we're getting on our customer satisfaction surveys and the comments we see on Yelp and other internet sites, customers are complaining about how uncomfortable the finance-office experience is. That can't help over the long haul. I think we need to look at some changes."

"Well, my people still have to check credit scores and discuss the financing options," Mike Leonard replies.

"Yeah, no one else can do that, but that's not what I'm talking about. I'm focused on the menu of extra warranties and other items," says Greg. "Why are they selling coverage for wheel damage? It's never made that much sense, and I don't think you want your finance office staff annoying the customers. You've got them sitting in an office while someone they just met looks up their credit score and any embarrassing details that might come out of that. Doesn't seem to me like an ideal opportunity to sell anybody a lifetime transmission warranty."

Greg obviously wants to make some changes. A few weeks earlier, he brought in a consultant to look at all the dealerships and offer ways to improve the customer experience and increase sales. Today's impromptu meeting looks like it might be something the consultant recommended.

"We don't have to keep grinding away at this. Here's what I want to do," he declares. It's pure Greg Allen—rapid-fire decision-making that seems to come right from his entrepreneurial spirit. He may have a loud personality, but he always stays on point.

The revenue from add-ons is essential.

"Let's refocus the finance-office role on *financing* and task our salespeople with selling add-ons along with all the other options. The salesroom seems like a better place to do that. But I don't want to go crazy here. First, let's make the change in our dealerships in Van Nuys and Cerritos and give it six months to see how it goes. I'm betting that we will see increased add-on sales in that environment. If it works, we can roll it out to our other dealerships.

"Our people are all going to hear about this, so we need to get out in front with the news of the change. Bob, can you or someone on your marketing team draft a letter for my signature that explains the changes to everyone in the company?"

You notice Bob looking straight at you as Greg says this. It seems clear that the assignment is coming your way.

"I want to make sure the finance people don't take it the wrong way," Greg explains. "We're not making this change because we think they've screwed up. Have them see it as clearing the decks so that they can focus on financing our customers' purchases. That's an important part of our revenue picture." He makes a sweeping gesture with his hand.

"And the sales guys need to understand that they're getting increased responsibility for the overall sales number on each vehicle purchase. They're pros, so that should come as welcome news. Tell them we will provide them with some training on add-on features and benefits. And although it's too early to get into the specifics, let them know that we will take a look at the sales bonus program to see how we might be able to sweeten the deal for them. But don't make any promises. I want to motivate them, but we need to see the results from Van Nuys and Cerritos first.

"Everyone should already know, but make it clear that our margins have really dropped on new vehicle sales. That's not some state secret. We're getting squeezed by internet-smart customers and the carmakers too. The revenue from the add-ons is essential. We need to change how we do business. I'm guessing a couple hundred words, but use your judgment on that, Bob. Just make sure it sends the right message to the whole team. Get it to me by the end of the week."

We'll take a look at the bonus program, but don't make any promises.

Then, with a grin on his face, he dismisses the group with "Now everybody get outta here and go back to work."

3

RIDING AN
UNEXPECTED WAVE

*Sending Assurance to Employees and
Franchisees to Counter Distracting News*

W*hat a lucky break*, you think as you pull your car into the employee parking lot at the Juice Joint. *I'm getting to use the accounting skills I learned at college, and I'm learning about the consumer business world and franchising operations. How good can it get?*

A May graduate, you earned a business administration degree with an accounting emphasis. The accounting professors put you through your paces in the coursework, and your internship at the Juice Joint paid off with a job offer from the rapidly growing company.

The Juice Joint Inc. has been on a tear recently. Started ten years ago by Theodore "Teddy" Driessen, who jokingly calls himself a "recovering surfer" from Seal Beach, the company

What are the important facts he'd want to use?

has expanded from one store in the South Bay to forty-two locations from Pismo Beach south to San Diego. More recently, the company opened stores in San Francisco, Denver, and Las Vegas. In addition to its traditional offerings of blended fruit juices, smoothies, and protein drinks, over the past year the Juice Joint has added its own brand of health-conscious snack foods like Krazee Kale Chips, which are selling well, and is testing a line of healthy lunch items to expand its menu.

I want you to keep your eye on the ball.

The company owns fifteen of its stores; the rest are run by franchisees. Total sales for the last fiscal year were slightly more than $14 million. Individual store sales are roughly $336,000, which is about average among comparable businesses. You were hired for a role in accounting, but since the corporate team is so small (everyone is in one office suite in a building on Ocean Park Boulevard in Santa Monica) you've had the chance to get involved in a range of activities, including marketing and even working with franchising operations. And Teddy Driessen is a great leader, always brimming with enthusiasm and new ideas to grow the business. The whole place is a hands-on learning environment for a new employee like you.

The Juice Joint is privately held, and Teddy owns about 41 percent of the outstanding shares. The company's chief financial officer, Muriel Spitz, owns another 10 percent. Muriel hired you as part of her financial team. Most of the remaining shares are held by Ron Carpenter, a wealthy developer and investor who is well known for the successful shopping centers and high-end resorts he's built around Southern California.

Carpenter has been a big supporter of the Juice Joint since the beginning, but more recently, he has been keenly interested in getting a better financial return on his investment. He has been quietly pressing Teddy for several months to go slow with his expansion plans. The new stores in San Francisco and Denver have yet to turn a profit in the very expensive markets they serve. And the new lines of snack products are also proving very costly. The planned expansion into a line of lunch meals would be another serious drag on profits, and Carpenter has finally put his foot down. He wants the Juice Joint to lower its expenses and improve the bottom line.

Last week, in an interview with the *Los Angeles Times* about his many and varied business interests, Carpenter directly challenged Teddy on the overhead expense levels at the Juice Joint, which he said "are way too high." He questioned the wisdom of Teddy's costly investments in new products and out-of-market store locations. "Juice Joint needs to stabilize the profitability of its current operations before they start chasing more growth," he was quoted as saying.

Teddy is not someone who backs down from an argument, even with a prominent investor. In a hastily arranged interview with *SoCal Business News* that appeared this morning, Teddy said that he always welcomed the "opinions of his investors" but that "the popularity and market momentum of the Juice Joint more than justifies the company's ongoing commitment to expansion. It would be irresponsible of me to slow down our very measured and deliberate plans while the Juice Joint is ideally positioned for continuing growth. There's no 'growth chasing' going on here."

With that, what had been a private discussion between Teddy and Carpenter became a very public dispute.

The franchisees and store employees are on the front line with customers.

Now, Teddy has called the small corporate staff together to tell them that he wants them to stay focused on their work and not be distracted by the dueling stories in the media or the disagreement between himself and Ron Carpenter. "Regardless of whether you work in store operations, franchise relations, marketing, accounting, or whatever, I want all of you to keep your eye on the ball. Some individuals may see me as nothing more than a surfer," Teddy says with an edge in his voice, "but I think I have a good feel for our marketplace. We will get past this and continue to build the Juice Joint brand." His enthusiastic tone has returned.

Then he gets serious again. "But I'm worried about the reaction from the people working in our stores and from our franchisees. They need to know that we are committed to our shared success

What are the important facts he'd want to use?

and that our growth plans are sound and attainable. We need all of them to stay focused on customer satisfaction and efficient retail-store management. They're going to see this stuff in the media—hell, they've probably already seen it. I don't want them to be distracted by all this.

"I'm going to call some of them now, but I want to send an email today to all our franchisees and store managers explaining what's going on and reinforcing my commitment to their success. They're the ones on the front line with our customers, delivering the quality products and first-rate service that are essential to the Juice Joint's future. They need to hear that from me."

And then, to your complete shock and surprise, Teddy turns to you and says, "I know you were hired to do accounting, but this is a small team, and you're a new college graduate—so you may be the best writer we have around this place. I want you to write that email and get it back to me today. I don't want all the people in those forty-two stores wondering what's going on with Juice Joint or worrying that we might be in trouble. Keep it crisp and on-point, but make sure it gets our message across. And it needs to sound like me—enthusiastic and committed."

What Teddy doesn't know is that you've never seen yourself as much of a writer. Back at school, you took that communications course, but only because the social media class you really wanted was full and you needed the credits to graduate.

Teddy needs to be tactful with Carpenter.

Where do I start, and what do I write? you think to yourself as you walk to your cubicle. You know Teddy wants it to sound like him but what does that mean —an enthusiastic surfer? He certainly doesn't want to scare anyone in the stores; he wants them to stay focused on their work, just like he told the corporate team in the all-hands meeting. What are the important facts he'd want to use to make his case? Are there facts or plans he wouldn't want to mention? Might the people in the stores or even the franchise owners somehow see Carpenter's emphasis on the Juice Joint's costs being "way too high" as a threat that could impact them? *How should I address that in Teddy's email?* you wonder.

You're also aware that Teddy can't call out Carpenter by name; the man still has a substantial ownership position in the company. Teddy may be annoyed with Carpenter now, but he needs to be tactful.

You sigh as you turn on your computer and let your mind wander for a moment. *Why didn't the university offer a course that might help with an assignment like this?* you ask yourself. Actually, maybe it did. You can't really remember. But there's no time for idle musing. Teddy usually leaves around six in the evening, and he'll want to see your draft long before then. You need to start writing.

4

IF THE SHOE FITS

Keeping the Sales Reps Focused on Future Opportunities, Not Past Successes

Sometimes things just seem to work out, or at least it appeared that way until today. The internship you scored with Pacers Inc. in your last year at the university evolved into a full-time job with the Marina del Rey–based athletic footwear company. Now you're a full-fledged member of the marketing team at the fast-growing company, but admittedly, the low person in the pecking order.

Pacers Inc. is a relative newcomer in the athletic-footwear category, but it's already in hot pursuit of the industry leaders, according to outside retail tracking services and Pacer's proprietary market research data. A big part of the company's success stems from the work of the company's marketing group, led by your hard-charging boss, Edith Wilton. Since Edith hired you a year ago, you've learned a ton from her about how to think like a marketer. The material that was covered in the marketing courses at school have clicked into place. It's now clear to you just how relevant all that stuff really was.

Pacers's sales are up more than $500M, a 40 percent increase in the last quarter, and it looks like it's going to be another record-breaking year for the

Demand for high-end athletic shoes is slowing and likely to plateau.

company. It hasn't all been smooth sailing however. PacerWear, a new line of warm-up gear and other athletic clothing introduced last year, is barely profitable. It's Pacer's first foray outside its core athletic shoe business and has seriously underperformed company expectations. The weak market reception is said to be partially attributable to a lack of focus on the new line among sales representatives. Edith is leading the charge to make sure that never happens again.

In addition, the company's market forecasts, supported by feedback from the sales team, indicate that the demand for high-end (and high-margin) athletic shoes is slowing and is likely to plateau in the near future. That has been the company's sweet spot, and the premium shoe lines are supported by extensive marketing promotions and high-profile, high-cost, endorsements from world-class athletes.

Most of the demand growth is now in the lower-priced, more affordable athletic-style footwear category. A number of new, affordable brands are pushing into the athletic-footwear category. Across the entire industry, this trend is being described as the *athleisure* product category. Pacer knows that it has to respond to these changing market dynamics, and a soon-to-be-announced product offering is designed to do just that.

The new LeisurePace product line offers customers a full range of competitively priced casual athletic shoes. Some of the shoes in the line are clearly intended for everyday wear or even for work in an office environment. Edith has had the entire marketing team working at developing a full-up plan to roll out the LeisurePace line, and a key plan element is an internal introduction of the new offering to the sales force.

Edith's concerns are twofold. First, nearly all the sales reps in the field are experienced in the area of high-performance footwear. The LeisurePace product line is going to require a different sales approach focused on the occasional athlete and customers who are just interested in comfortable, attractively styled shoes. Second, last year's PacerWear experience clearly demonstrated the need to make certain that the sales reps are entirely on board with the new product offering.

Rather than wait for the annual sales meeting later this year to launch sales-force training on the new line, Edith has decided that the

LeisurePace internal introduction will kick off with a webinar for the entire national sales team in advance of the annual meeting. Every sales rep will receive a LeisurePace kit prior to the webinar with the following:

- specifics about the product offering
- a PowerPoint summary of the market forces driving the company's push into the athleisure category
- a detailed calendar of advertising and promotional activities
- special product information that will be available on the reps' company-provided iPads for use during sales calls
- pricing sheets
- the specifics of a special sales incentive (i.e., bonus) program for LeisurePace sales orders
- a T-shirt that the reps will be encouraged to wear to the webinar that boldly declares, "I'm setting the pace with LeisurePace!"

Along with the rest of the team, you've been totally immersed in the LeisurePace project for months now. Edith has let you participate at every step along the way as the entire marketing program was developed, including the internal introduction kit and webinar. She obviously believes you are a high-potential employee with a bright and promising future with Pacer. You are determined to make sure she keeps thinking that way.

Make it crystal clear that the company is 100 percent behind this new product line.

But today, you are caught flat-footed (never a good thing in the footwear business) when Edith comes to your desk with a special request.

"Look," she says, "the advance kits are going to be shipped out next Monday, and there's one remaining component that I want you to prepare. We need a hard-hitting cover letter on the front of the kit from Phil Rothstein." Phil is the company's founder and CEO.

Edith continues, "Phil has never done that before, but he thinks it's a good idea. He wants to make it crystal clear to all the sales reps that the company is 100 percent behind this new product line, up and down the entire organization. The letter doesn't have to be long, but it does have to deliver Phil's key message clearly and comprehensively. And it doesn't have to plow through all the content in the kit or the webinar. That's not his role. The key thing is to underscore the strong support the LeisurePace line has at the top of the company, the enthusiasm about the new product offering, and the confidence we have that it's going to be a winner in a changing industry landscape."

Before she turns to go, Edith adds, "Athleisure products are the future, and we have to make sure that Pacer is a part of that future. That's what LeisurePace represents for us. You've been involved with this project for almost the entire year you've been with the company. At this point, I'm certain you have the understanding and the product knowledge to take care of this for me and for Phil."

How do these things happen? you ask yourself as Edith walks away. *I'm one year out of college, and now they want me to write for the CEO?* As a third-year student at the university, you took the management communications course from that guy with the name you never could spell. Now you can't even remember it. The weekly writing assignments were tedious and time-consuming, but you slogged through the course, got a B, and then promptly moved on. And now this!

> *Athleisure products are the future. That's what LeisurePace represents.*

What was it that Edith said? *Enthusiasm. Confidence. Strong corporate support. The future. Deliver Phil's key message clearly. Don't plow through all the details.* She almost made it sound urgent that the LeisurePace product line becomes a smashing success. You suppose you can do this; plus, she really didn't leave you with a choice about it.

Over the past year, Edith has been your strongest supporter and even a mentor, although you never actually talked about that with her. You don't want to let her down now. She's demonstrating the faith she has in you. You have to make good on her belief.

5

STAY THE COURSE AND STAY POSITIVE

Projecting Determination and Overcoming Employee Doubts in a Tough Market

In a real sense, Broward's Department Stores Inc. is the only place you've ever worked. With the exception of a brief stint as a restaurant server while in high school, it's been Broward's ever since you started as a Christmas season salesclerk while a first-year college student. You worked part-time through all four years, and to no one's surprise accepted their offer of a management trainee position after graduating two years ago.

Since then, you've spent time in store management, buying, and inventory management. Your final six-month rotating assignment has been as an assistant to the chief financial officer, George Haskill. You never styled yourself a numbers person, but it's been valuable to see the company through the lens of the finance department's spreadsheets and schedules.

George has been terrific. He's made every effort to involve you in all aspects of his role, and you have a far greater appreciation now of the fact that the CFO is not just the person who reports the financial results every quarter. George is a key player in setting the strategy for the company, along with CEO Jeff Broward. Jeff is the fourth generation in his family to lead the business.

Broward's is in many respects an anomaly in the current retailing world: an independent, regionally based department store. It began with Jakob Brodsky, an immigrant from Russia, who started as a peddler selling fabrics, sewing needles, buttons, ribbons, and threads from his pushcart until he scraped together enough money to open his first store under his new, anglicized name of Broward.

The store prospered at its first location in Long Beach, California, and in the post–World War II years, Broward's followed its customers

Some observers have described the changes as a "retail apocalypse."

to the new malls, opening additional stores in Fullerton, Yorba Linda, Santa Ana, and Pomona. Broward's product offering focused on mid-priced goods combined with the top-notch customer service typically found in high-end stores like Nordstrom's or Bloomingdale's. The family lore was that Jakob treated every customer who bought from his cart with the greatest respect and attentiveness, whether they bought ten yards of velvet fabric or just a couple of buttons. The catchphrase "a couple of buttons" still animates Broward's culture of customer service almost a century later.

That same sense of respect and attentiveness carries through the company and can even be found in the courteous way Broward's people treat each other in their interactions. It is a good place to work, which helps explain why you were attracted to the company.

No one would say that the larger department-store world is in a good place, however. The entire industry is confronting serious upheaval. Fewer people are shopping in malls across the nation, including Southern California. And the explosive rise of e-commerce, especially Amazon and other digital outlets, has led to a brutal shakeout. The big department store chains have closed thousands of stores nationwide. More ominously, local department stores like Broward's have gone out of business at an alarming rate. Some observers have described the changes as a "retail apocalypse."

Broward's has not stood still in the face of the threatening changes to the marketplace. Jeff, along with George, has closely managed costs across the business. They have resisted the

The headline leaves the long-term outlook open to speculation.

temptation to open more stores like some of their competitors, who did so and are now financially overextended or out of business.

Broward's did spend substantially to upgrade the appearance of its five stores. And it invested in a completely overhauled website that provides customers with the ease of e-commerce combined with same-day or next day shipping from the physical store location in its service area. The online promotional promise offers "Selection, Speed, and the *Attentive* Service You Expect from Broward's." It is "a couple of buttons" for the digital age, Jeff has quipped.

The company has empowered its employees at every store to accept the return of merchandise purchased online for an exchange, refund, or credit. And it's exhorted the entire workforce to think and act with the agility of a start-up business. Digital sales, which were virtually nonexistent a few years ago, now account for more than 10 percent of Broward's annual sales, and Jeff has set a target of 25 percent in three years.

Despite all the effort to grow the business and contain costs, it's still been challenging. Revenue has increased steadily over the past two years, but earnings over the same period fell 20 percent, largely due to the expense of upgrading the stores; building and operating the website; and making slightly larger advertising expenditures.

A headline in this morning's *Los Angeles Times* captures the entire story: "Broward's Stumbles Despite Strong Efforts." The story outlines all the management initiatives that Jeff has launched and describes in

We have a distinctive culture that we need to cherish and sustain.

detail the new website and its potential to increase sales. But the article also notes the earnings slump and threats facing Broward's along with every other brick-and-mortar store in the changing retail marketplace.

"There's nothing actually wrong or factually incorrect about the story," Jeff says with a note of irritation in his voice. "But the headline sounds dire, and the article leaves our long-term outlook open to speculation. I think we have a good handle on the situation, and we can continue to make progress if we stay focused and not let ourselves get distracted by all the noise and by stories like this."

He is sitting at his desk, the newspaper spread open in front of him. George sits across from Jeff. He is there to review the financials for the last month and the revised outlook for the quarter and the full year. As he often does, George has brought you along with some other members of his finance team. "Just listen to the conversations," he tells you. "You'll get a good understanding of how the numbers shape Jeff's approach to the business." But the newspaper story got things going in a different direction.

"I know you agree with me, George," Jeff says. "We're taking the right approach. We just have to keep a close watch on our costs, press ahead with our e-commerce strategy, and run the stores too! If we start looking over our shoulders and second-guessing ourselves, then for sure we'll stumble, just like the headline says."

He continues, "I want to send an email to everyone in the company this morning. They'll already have seen this story, or they will hear about it shortly. We don't want to run away from it even if we could. Our message needs to be that Broward's has a promising future even in times like this. We are building on a great tradition. We have a distinctive store culture that we need to cherish and sustain. And we have an understanding of what we need to do going forward. Some specifics should be included, but I want the overall message to be that we're on the right path and we need everyone to pull together to secure our future. Please see if you can get someone on your team to knock out a draft in the next hour or so. I don't want this story to linger without a response from us to the entire workforce."

We're on the right path and need everyone to pull together.

Inwardly, you smile to yourself to hear Jeff say *please* even in a situation like this. It is so typical of Broward's people, and it underscores the fact that he really does set the tone that infuses the store's culture.

George quickly goes through the financial reports and leaves them with Jeff, saying he'll stop by at lunchtime to discuss them in more detail. The meeting ends shortly afterward. Back down the hall in the finance staff meeting room, George turns to you and asks you to draft an email to show Jeff. "I believe you know what it needs to say, so give it your best effort. Use your judgment on how long it should be. Then, you and I will get back with Jeff to review what we have. Thanks."

6

FLYING FRUSTRATION

Winning Back Your Customers' Trust

So far, it's been an ideal job. As a junior staffer in the customer-relations department at GlobalHorizon Airlines, you've had an opportunity to apply some of what you learned as a business-management major while also enjoying a close connection with flying and aircraft, things that have fascinated you since your parents first took you to an air show as a child. But after more than three years, you're looking for a way to advance in your career.

That's something you made known to your boss, Marilyn Strout, the director of customer relations, during your most recent performance review. During that session, Marilyn said you were a "strong performer" and "promotable," but she said nothing about a possible new role with greater responsibilities. You were left wondering.

Despite its ambitious name, GlobalHorizon is a midsized carrier based in Phoenix, Arizona, with a network of US domestic air routes as well as destinations in Canada, Mexico, and the Caribbean. The company operates a fleet of nearly 130 Airbus planes and has about seven thousand employees. The company promotes itself

A Discount Airline with a Difference.

as "A Discount Airline with a Difference," and that difference—the thing that GlobalHorizon wants to use to differentiate itself from the competition—is first-rate customer relations. "We're not here just to take the incoming complaints," Marilyn always says. "Our job is to make sure that our passengers have a quality flying experience on board our planes."

To that end, the customer-relations team isn't focused entirely on managing the call center and fielding customer problems and complaints. It also manages the Global Aviator frequent-flyer program in coordination with the sales team, conducts regular customer-satisfaction surveys, and sponsors frequent customer-experience workshops with pilots, flight attendants, agents, ground crew, and mechanics to keep everyone in the company aligned with the goal of pleasing the customer. "Customer satisfaction is *everyone's* job!" read the buttons and banners Marilyn has had distributed across the entire organization. But as with any large, complex company with millions of customer interactions, things don't always go according to plan.

Get something to me by
tomorrow.

Marilyn came to your desk today with three angry emails addressed to the chairman and CEO, Buzz Olsen, concerning a recent flight. One of the emails was especially indignant. A Mr. Chris Marlowe, who was most likely a business executive, explained that he was a Platinum Aviator, the highest level in the frequent-flyer program, with nearly two million miles in his Global Aviator account. Frequent flyers are especially desirable customers. While they make up only a relatively small percentage of all flyers, they contribute a disproportionately large share of every airline's revenue. The other two customers, Ms. Francine Jansen and Mr. Jack Donne, appeared to be leisure travelers without Global Aviator accounts.

All three expressed frustration about having been bumped from the oversold morning flight, and they were not placated by the standard compensation they were offered, even though all three were booked on another flight late that afternoon. Reportedly, some harsh words were directed at the gate agent, according to two TSA workers who were on a break nearby and observed the situation. The agent kept her cool, but all three passengers loudly proclaimed that they would never again fly on GlobalHorizon Airlines. In addition to his email, Jack Donne posted some very negative comments on several websites visited by vast numbers of airline ticket buyers.

Overbooking is a form of overselling that occurs in highly volatile markets where inventory cannot be stored. The overselling helps offset the no-shows that might result in empty seats on a flight. (Hotel rooms are another classic example of inventory that can't be stored and are also subject to overbooking.) Airline overbooking is allowed, but the US government has compensation levels for passengers who find themselves bumped due to overbooking. Basically, involuntarily bumped passengers for whom there is no substitute transportation available to get them to their destination in less than two hours of their scheduled arrival qualify for compensation of 400 percent of their one-way fare.[13]

"Look," Marilyn said, "I want you to draft the email replies that Buzz can send to these passengers. Try to get something to me by tomorrow or the following day. Obviously, we want to apologize for the problem and the inconvenience. Touch on the policy for overbooked flights. And, most importantly, try to re-earn their good will and repeat business. That's a tall order, but I think the key will be the tone that we use in our replies. We'll know if we succeeded if Mr. Donne updates his angry post on that consumer website."

> *Given his Platinum Aviator status, we need to take special care of Marlowe.*

She added, "Also, given his status as a Platinum Aviator, we need to take special care of Marlowe. Instead of a letter, put together talking points that Buzz can use in a phone call with him. That might be the best way to bring him around to a more positive attitude about the airline."

You had the impression that Marilyn's comment about getting Donne to revise his website post wasn't a jest. And you noticed that she didn't give you any guidance on whether these three

> *Why did Marilyn give you this assignment?*

---

[13] A summary of the US Department of Transportation policy on passenger bumping is in the appendix.

customers should be offered further compensation due to the extraordinary circumstances of their bumping. But it's obvious that the tone of the drafts should focus on the airline's concern about the inconvenience each customer experienced. You're not quite sure where to go on the issue of added compensation, but you think it best to make an offer of travel vouchers in your draft letter and wait for Marilyn to review the draft and makes a final decision.

You're also not certain how much detail to provide about bumping policies, although your instincts are telling you that short and sweet is probably best for the emails. The talking points for the phone call with the Platinum Aviator would need to be more accommodating, given his status as a regular customer.[14]

But the larger question in your mind is, why did Marilyn give you this assignment in the first place? The customer-relations team already had standard language for letters and emails like this. Was it because the customers had written directly to Buzz? Or might this assignment have something to do with your expressed desire to advance in your career and the promotable rating she gave you in that recent review? Could she actually be testing you?

---

[14] See the appendix for a guide to writing talking points.

7

DON'T EASE UP ON THE GAS

Getting Everyone Ready for a Market Downturn

One step at a time, you thought to yourself as you passed the one-year mark at SoCal Motors Inc. in Torrance. It had taken more than eight long months to land a suitable job after graduating from college. But you finally did, and it's been great.

SoCal Motors is one of California's largest automotive operations, with dealerships across the Los Angeles region offering domestic and imported vehicles. Your job on the small market research and analytics team has given you exposure to the broader trends shaping the automotive and truck market. As the most junior member of the three-person team, you've had to do all the slogging through the data the various manufacturers provide as well as macro stuff from other sources, while the actual analysis is done by the others. It can be tedious at times, but you're learning the industry and how a real company uses market-research data for revenue forecasting, setting sales targets, and setting budgets.

Plus, your boss, Jim Hopkins, the longtime director of market analysis, seems to like you. In many important ways, he's teaching you the business. Jim is smart, knowledgeable, enthusiastic, blunt, and occasionally profane.

The company experienced a shock to the system shortly after you were hired. Jonathan Franklin, the CEO and founder, was killed while racing cars in Germany. Many employees thought the company might be broken up and sold off in parts, which would have been bad news for the small corporate group in Torrance—especially you as a lowly new hire. But his widow, Mary, stepped into the CEO role, and despite whispered doubts and skepticism from some of the old "car guys," she's shown herself to be a capable and decisive leader.

We're looking at a tougher market near-term.

It helped that in her first year as CEO, the industry enjoyed sustained demand, especially for SUVs and trucks. The combined sales volume for the entire US market for cars and trucks, known in the industry as the SAAR (seasonally adjusted annual sales rate), calculated monthly, reached a record 18 million vehicles last year. This calendar year, the first year that Mary Franklin was leading SoCal Motors, the SAAR was 17.5 million. That was a very healthy industrywide sales number by historic standards, though still behind the previous year.

But now, the estimated SAAR for the coming year is expected to come in at 17.45 million units sold. That is still good volume, but the US market clearly seems to have peaked. And there are other signs of a slowdown. The two leading players in the industry are reporting retail sales drops at their dealerships. Sales incentives (basically discounts) per vehicle sold were up 11 percent over the past year across the industry and were now more than $3,000 per vehicle sold.

If retail sales weakness continues, carmakers are going to have to do more to increase those discounts and probably cut their production levels as well. It just doesn't seem like the market can absorb all the vehicles being manufactured. The recent monthly new-car sales results for the big manufacturers mostly showed declines. Only one car company showed a modest 1.1 percent increase, which is basically flat. Five others recorded declines, in one case by a whopping 18 percent.

"It's hard to say whether this is just a temporary pause in market growth, a sustained slowdown, or even the start of a falloff in industry-wide sales," Jim explains. He is briefing Mary Franklin in her office on the new market data before sending his monthly business outlook and forecast to all the dealerships in the SoCal Motors group. He has brought you along as your reward for doing the PowerPoints. "But we're looking at a tougher market near-term," he says. "That much is certain."

He pauses and looks straight at Mary. "I don't want to sound overly cynical, but there's something else that's pretty certain. Most of the general managers at our dealerships have been through this before, and some of them might just be inclined to try to ride out a down cycle without taking any special actions to confront a sales slump."

What he leaves unsaid is that some of the general managers might hunker down and wait to see what Mary does when confronted by a softening market. In a sense, they will be testing her.

"You need to get out there and make damn sure those dealership general managers don't simply throw up their hands and say there's nothing they can do if the market deteriorates," he tells her.

No one's going to throw up their hands, especially me.

"No one's going to throw up their hands," Mary replies with a smile on her face, "especially me. I'm going to meet with the GM of every dealership and review plans to manage any possible sales declines. I specifically want to get their plans to grow their service and maintenance revenue to offset a decline in vehicle sales and also their contingency plans to reduce their operating costs and expense levels.

"On that point, I want to see detailed cost-cutting plans based on sales decline scenarios of 5 percent, 10 percent, and 15 percent. They should work with Tom Hampton and his guys in finance to develop the numbers. And, finally, I want to hear any ideas they have for special promotional programs at their dealerships."

Wow, you think to yourself. *Mary Franklin really knows what she's doing and what she wants done.*

"Before I set up those meetings with each GM, Jim," Mary continues, "I want you to send your usual monthly business

We need to face this softening in the market with determination and confidence.

outlook detailing the challenges we are facing—but this time, include a letter from me explaining the things that I will expect to review with each of them in person over the next few weeks."

"That's a great idea, Mary, but you sure as hell don't want me to draft that letter," says Jim. "I'd probably make it too blunt and edgy. It would just scare some of them and annoy the rest."

"OK," she agrees. "Who would you recommend to write it?"

"I think our writer is sitting over there," Jim replies as he glances over to you.

Mary turns, looks directly at you, and asks, "Do you want to draft the letter?"

"Sure," you say, all the while hoping she doesn't hear the uncertainty in your voice.

This is a time for strong and decisive leadership.

"You've heard what I want to cover," Mary says. "Briefly outline the market situation that Jim will detail in his monthly outlook report. Don't make it gloomy, however. The tone is really important. I don't want it to sound like the sky is falling. We need to face this softening in the market with determination and confidence. Tell them that my administrative assistant will contact each of them shortly to set up a meeting where we will review the plans every dealership will have in place to manage a drop in new car and truck sales.

"You know what I'm interested in getting from them. This is a time for strong and decisive leadership, and that's exactly what I expect from every dealership general manager. We don't want anyone to take their foot off the gas. I'm not certain of the length, but give the message what it's worth. And try to get your draft to me tomorrow."

And just like that, the meeting is over. "OK, I think that's it for now," Mary says as she rises from her chair. You follow Jim out of her office, already thinking about the assignment you just received from the company president and the very short deadline that came with it.

8

SAD NEWS,
BUT STAY FOCUSED

Highlighting the Business, Not the Individual

Four years out of college, and things have gone well—at least until recently. You landed the job with the Beachcomber Group not long after graduation, and it's been an interesting forty-eight months. The LA-based company was founded more than twenty-five years ago as a pioneering start-up in the organic, natural foods, and personal-care-product categories. Its Match Point brand cold-pressed juices, Good Earth veggie chips, Wholesome Nature herbal teas, and Malibu Breeze lotions and skin-care products are distributed to supermarkets and convenience stores as well as restaurants throughout the western United States.

Across the entire product line, the Beachcomber brand combines the healthy image of organic products with the laid-back vibe of a Southern California lifestyle. In fact, the company's origin story (or myth, depending on what you choose to believe) is that the inspiration to start the company came to its founder, Russ Chatham, a New York transplant, on his first day in Los Angeles as he walked along the sands of Hermosa Beach determined to devote his life to surfing and beach volleyball.

Whether the story is entirely true (Russ already had an MBA and experience working in marketing for a New York bagel company before he fled the cold weather for Southern California) is less important than the fact that he's been an inspiring and charismatic leader. He's consistently been open and engaged with staff across the company and at every level of the organization. His infectious enthusiasm and big plans for the future have caught the imagination of just about everyone who works at Beachcomber. And he consistently tries to develop people and support them in growing their careers.

Certainly, that's been your experience. Russ has had a major impact on your career and your understanding of business. Although you officially report to Jolene Conrad, the chief marketing officer, for the past two years you've essentially served as an aide to Russ, working on his presentations and doing the advance work for meetings in conjunction with Jolene's marketing team and chief financial officer Jane Smyth's finance team.

It's been a terrific learning experience as the company grew. Sales for the last fiscal year exceeded $1 billion, but recently some troubling trends suggest difficult times ahead for both revenues and profits.

There have been a few significant stumbles as well. Russ's strategic moves into new product categories—Authentic Farm brand organic pet food and Free 'n' Natural brand baby food—have yet to meet with much success. Both product lines have been a drain on the company's finances and management attention. They have been consistent money-losers in the two years since their launch. And they are highly visible contributors to the downward pressure on the company's profit margins and its high marketing and distribution costs.

Compounding these new-product-introduction difficulties, there's intensifying competition across all the product lines. When Russ started Beachcomber, organic foods and personal-care items were still niche product offerings. There were few competitors in the organic space, and the big packaged-food companies weren't really paying much attention to the relatively small market for organics. That has changed dramatically over the past decade or so. Today's market is filled with new organic-product start-up companies. And the big guys finally caught up with the growing customer demand for organics and introduced their own organic product lines, backed up with all their financial strength and marketing muscle. Beachcomber's margins have suffered from increasing market pressure.

There have been very loud complaints from some of the company's investors that Russ has overreached and pushed the Beachcomber Group into product categories where it has virtually no experience. The last annual shareholders' meeting brought the issue into full public view. Major investors demanded that Beachcomber retrench, sell off money-losing operations like Authentic Farm and Free 'n' Natural, reduce its overall expense levels, and get the company back to sustained profitability.

There were even calls for Russ to resign. Others said that the Beachcomber Group should be broken up and sold off piecemeal.

The headquarters office in El Segundo has been filled with tension the last few weeks. Russ's office door has been closed for hours on end—a new development for a leader who had always prided himself on his open-door policy. Many of those closed-door sessions have involved Jane Smyth and Edward Furrow, the company's general counsel, along with several outside lawyers and bankers he brought with him. Even some of the major shareholders who spoke at the annual meeting have been seen in the executive office area. Obviously, something is up.

Investments in new product development and marketing to defend our core-product lines.

It's a late Friday afternoon, and Russ has called you into his office. In the past, he has often used this time to talk about his dreams for the future of Beachcomber. But now he seems tired and deflated. The pressures of the past several weeks are clearly wearing him down, even though he smiles and tries to sound upbeat.

We can't have everyone sitting around speculating about the changes.

"Look," he says, "it's probably been pretty obvious that the company has been under a lot of strain. Our large shareholders are really pounding the table about the need for major changes, and frankly, some of our own guys think we've bitten off more than we can chew with our new product offerings. I suppose I have to agree with them. So, on Monday, we're going to announce several major changes.

"First, we will sell the Authentic Farm and Free 'n' Natural lines. We're never going to get any traction competing with those big pet food operations. The same with the major baby food companies that just have more product equity than we can build up without a tremendous expenditure, even in the organic space.

"We will also be taking a look at our entire cost structure to see where we can generate savings. We're going to need those funds to make investments in new product development and marketing to defend our core juice, tea, snack, and personal-care product lines in a tough market environment.

"Finally, I'm going to be stepping down as CEO and assisting the board in recruiting a new leader to take the company forward."

There is no emotion in his voice, but you can see that this last bit of news hurts. Beachcomber is his life's work.

There are good people all across the company.

"The announcement of all this is being handled by Jane's investor-relations people and Ed's legal guys. It needs to be done by the book. We don't want to pull a Twitter stunt and just toss the news out there on social media like some politician."

He adds, "But there is one thing you could do for me. I want to use our videoconferencing capability to speak with all our team members on Monday. And I do mean *everyone*, from the leaders and managers to the sales force, product managers, and folks in the distribution centers. Everyone. They need to know several things.

"Obviously, there's the news itself, along with why we're making these changes. But I also want them to know that over the years, they have all shared in the effort to make Beachcomber the success that it is. And, just as importantly, I need them to stay focused on doing their jobs and to not let all the changes distract them.

"Human nature being what it is, I know that's a tall order. But Beachcomber can't afford to have everyone sitting around speculating about the changes or about a new leader. There are good people all across the company, and they are part of Beachcomber's future. They need to understand that.

"I know this is all very sudden, but I'd like you to prepare some well-developed talking points I can use that make my message clear and hit all the key points. I don't want to get caught up in the moment and miss anything important. The right tone will be critical. While this is a business matter, I also see this as my personal message. I want everyone to come away with a sense of confidence in the future of the organization. And I definitely don't want the focus on *me*! This isn't what I wanted, but I'll be OK.

I want everyone to come away with a sense of confidence in the future.

I just want everyone to do what they can to make sure that *Beachcomber* is OK.

"It doesn't have to be long, so use your judgment. Make it as long as it needs to be to get the message across. Get the draft to me by Sunday morning, and also send copies to Ed and Jane. They need to make sure that it aligns with their efforts. And listen, I'm going to be around for a while, so this isn't goodbye. But I want you to know that you've been a great addition to our team. Thanks."

9

WHAT GETS MEASURED GETS DONE

Letting Your Prospective Employees Know Diversity Matters

You always thought that you'd like working in human resources—and now, eighteen months into your job as an HR generalist with NxGen360, you're more certain than ever. An internet marketing company located in Playa Vista, California, NxGen360 has been a great place to work and to learn. In large part, that's been due to the leadership of Jerry Madsen, a Stanford grad who broke the mold and left Silicon Valley to come home to Southern California to build his start-up.

Since he founded the company in 2011, Jerry has been a high-profile advocate for helping small and medium-sized companies take full advantage of internet-based opportunities for growth. A charismatic, forward-thinking leader, he's been featured in prominent publications like *Inc.* and *Fast Company* for his visionary approach to business.

The entire industry is criticized for its tech-bro culture.

NxGen360 offers a range of services to its clients, including search-engine optimization, social media marketing, pay-per-click services, qualified-lead generation, and online reputation management. The company has been growing like crazy. In the short time you've been there, annual revenues have reached $34 million, a 36 percent increase in a year and a half.

Hiring is trying to keep pace with business growth. That's given you, as the junior member of the small HR staff, extensive hands-on experience in the recruiting process and onboarding of new hires. And since human resources is a flat organization, you've had plenty of exposure to HR team leader Jessica McCarthy. Jerry avoids more traditional titles, and nearly everyone is simply called a team member or team leader.

Since you joined the company, the principal HR challenge has been recruiting. The competition is fierce for qualified software engineers, web developers, and similarly skilled prospects. Although it's often assumed that most applicants would find working in a small, fast-growing start-up like NxGen360 appealing, a surprising number still prefer the perceived glamour of the high-profile search or social media companies like Google or Facebook.

In addition, the entire tech industry is frequently criticized for its tech-bro culture and the low percentages of women and minority employees. Jessica has often expressed her concern about this issue. But the criticism gained far more urgency when Jerry appeared on a panel at a recent industry conference. The issue of diversity in recruiting and promotion came up unexpectedly in a question from the audience. All the panel members were roundly criticized for the poor performance of their companies in their hiring and promotion practices.

When Jerry returned from the conference, he was perplexed. "Ever since we started NxGen360, I've always wanted our ranks open to all enthusiastic and engaged job candidates," he told Jessica. "Get me the diversity metrics on our team members." When she reported back to him a few days later, the numbers were disappointing. It was obvious that NxGen360 had a long way to go to improve its hiring practices.

Aside from a few questions, Jerry said little when Jessica reviewed the findings and handed him the report. He seldom was that subdued about anything, and she didn't know how to read his reaction. But today it is clear that Jerry Madsen is determined to meet this challenge with the same level of intensity and determination he brought to every issue facing NxGen360.

He's called a meeting with Jessica and her entire HR team along with his key operations leader and general counsel. After everyone squeezes into the small conference room next to his workspace (no one at NxGen360 has

These are steep goals, but the jobs are going to be there.

formal offices, including Jerry), he pulls out the report and declares, "This is totally unacceptable. We can't continue to accept these pathetically poor numbers. I take responsibility for not being more attentive to the issue, but now I need the help and commitment of everyone in this room to fix the problem. In fact, it's not clear to me that this is a problem as much as it's an opportunity. If we can really pick up our game with diversity and inclusion, it'll go a long way to help with our overall hiring goals. Recruiting diverse candidates needs to be understood as *integral* to our company's growth, a vital part of our success going forward.

"So now it's a question of how we move forward. Here's what I think we should do to get the effort underway: Jessica, for the job fair in downtown LA next month and others coming up in San Jose and in Las Vegas in conjunction with the trade shows, I'd like to see a new recruiting information packet prepared that underscores our commitment to diversity in our hiring practices. The same materials can be used at all your scheduled campus recruiting visits too.

"Let's emphasize that NxGen360 is a great place to find opportunities to learn and to advance in your career. It should be made clear to everyone we meet in those sessions that we're a company that provides support and mentorship to our employees. As a member of the NxGen360 team, you're not just another cog in a machine.

"We're still a small enough organization that we can personalize the recruiting experience. For example, if a candidate advances in the hiring process to the point where you invite them to visit us here in Playa Vista, we should

NextGen360 is going to be out front on this.

encourage them to bring their spouse or significant other along for the visit. We want everyone we're interested in to feel comfortable with NxGen360. I think this is especially important with candidates who don't see themselves well represented in our industry. Now, what additional ideas do you guys have that can address this opportunity?"

The conversation continues for another thirty minutes, with everyone throwing out ideas that Jessica asks you to transcribe on the conference-room whiteboard. Then Jerry speaks again.

"Listen," he says, "we have some good stuff here. Now I want Jessica and her team to flesh it out into a plan. But we all know that our good intentions won't mean much if we don't have explicit and measurable goals. What gets measured, gets done.

"So, I want to put some numbers out there that NxGen360 will pledge to achieve. We'll make that pledge to our current team members, to the candidates we hope to recruit, and to the wider public. I never want to sit on another tech-industry panel and get hammered for doing nothing in this area.

"Over the next thirty months at NxGen360, the number of women and minority team leaders and associate team leaders will reach 20 percent, up from the current 12 percent. And over the same time frame, total NxGen360 diversity employment should rise to 25 percent from the current 16 percent These are some steep goals, but with the continued growth that we are projecting, the jobs are going to be there. We're just going to have to mount a serious and sustained campaign to find the right candidates to fill those jobs.

"Jessica, get your crew to work drafting that plan and the recruiting package we can use at upcoming job fairs and campus visits. Also, I'd like a letter prepared for my signature that addresses our commitment to having a diverse and inclusive workforce. We can include it with our recruitment materials. Have it portray the kind of company NxGen360 is, the growth we are experiencing, our encouraging and supportive culture, and the opportunities for learning and advancement that we offer. And include

Portray our growth, our supportive culture, and opportunities to advance.

those goals that we have set too; what gets measured gets done! Have the draft to me by next Friday. Don't focus on the length, but make sure that it covers all the points we want to make. NxGen360 is going to be out front on this."

As everyone leaves, Jessica asks the HR team to stay behind to discuss the assignment they just received. "Look," she says as she turns to you, "there's a bunch of things we need to work through to be ready for next Friday. I want you to focus on drafting that letter for Jerry. You heard the points he wants to emphasize.

"And," she says with a smile, "you're probably closest in age to the people he's trying to reach with his message. I'd like to see your draft by next Tuesday so that I have some time to read it and think it over. OK?"

10

CHANGE IS ON THE MENU

*Linking Changing Market Expectations
with Consistent Company Values*

It hadn't started exactly as you'd expected. There you were, a newly minted university graduate with your degree in business administration, struggling through your first days on the job in front of a scorching hot grill at a Burger Bistro. Eight burger patties at a time, trying to remember to set the timer for the fries, the lunch crowd filling the restaurant, and the store manager watching your every move—you remember thinking, *Things can only get better!*

Fortunately, they did. Working for at least two weeks on a counter and kitchen assignment in one of the company's stores was part of the Burger Bistro Way, the company philosophy developed by its founder, Saul Bernstein. He insisted that every new employee start at one of the stores making and serving burgers, fries, soft drinks, milkshakes, and other menu items to gain an appreciation for the fundamentals of the business and a better understanding of its customers.

Since those first weeks in the kitchen, you've rotated through several departments: human resources, purchasing/inventory management, store operations, marketing and branding, and accounting. And now you are on your last rotational assignment in the leadership office (LO) at the headquarters in downtown Los Angeles. Every assignment has been interesting, but the LO is giving you exposure to all the top people in the organization: Saul, the CEO and founder; CFO Eileen White; CIO Don DeAngelis; CMO Gabe Deluca; Senior Vice President for Store Operations Joan Dumont; and many more key people. It's a great opportunity to get to know them and to watch them operate. You're also very aware of the fact that it's an opportunity for them to watch you and get an impression of how valuable you might be to the organization. *No pressure here!* you thought to yourself on your first day in the LO.

We need to improve, and that means change.

Burger Bistro has been running at full speed since Saul started the company in Los Angeles in 2003. It quickly became one of the hottest businesses in the fast-casual dining sector of the restaurant industry. There are now ninety-three stores throughout the United States and Canada, with plans to expand to Japan, Hong Kong, Singapore, and Dubai.

Not that there haven't been challenges. Burger Bistro, like most of its competitors, is facing weaker foot traffic and higher labor costs. And same-store sales (i.e., the difference in revenue generated at an existing store over a certain period, usually a quarter, compared to the same period in the prior year) have dropped nearly 2 percent in the last quarter. The company recently announced that same-store sales would be down for the full year. The same-store sales metric is used by managers and investors to evaluate a retail company's performance and its outlook for the future. On top of that, Burger Bistro's stock is down, and Wall Street investors are starting to question whether the company can live up to its ambitious plans.

Despite these challenges, Saul Bernstein remains committed to the company's growth and long-term success. "Burger Bistro is one of the strongest brands in our market niche. Our customers are loyal to us and we're loyal to them," he insists. "The finest-quality top-notch service, fair prices, and distinctive menu offerings: those are the core values of the Burger Bistro Way."

Saul is speaking to a leadership meeting at headquarters. All the key executives are with him around the conference table, and you're seated along the wall, having already passed out copies of the most recent financial results and the other leadership reports. You're also there to help with the PowerPoint slides. (At this point, you're no longer amazed by how often these top executives screw up their own slide presentations.)

"Obviously, we need to improve in a number of ways, and that means *change*," Saul continues. "But we have to be smart about it and focused. I know all of you have ideas about how we can change, improve, and drive results. We can't do all of them at once, but there are a few I want us to work on first *and* work on as a team.

"For starters, I really think we need to focus on a shared idea that Eileen and Don have proposed. It has two main components. First, we want to strengthen our internal processes using Don's technology resources to more effectively support inventory, invoicing, and other financial systems that Eileen is responsible for. Second, we want to leverage our technology to connect us with our customers as we continue to expand.

Keep more revenue that's going to pickup-and-delivery apps.

"A mobile app that lets customers skip lines regardless of whether they order a takeout meal or plan to eat in our dining areas is what's needed. Plenty of restaurants are bringing mobile-app ordering into their businesses, but the key is to make one that's user friendly and reliable. Many of our competitors' apps are tricky to use and fail to complete orders accurately and on time. If we can develop an app that meets customers' expectations, it will make a major contribution to our growth and success. And it will let us keep more of the revenue that now goes to the pickup-and-delivery apps.

"At the same time, we need to pay close attention to our brand. I'd like Gabe to move forward with his proposal to team up with Joan and her store-management people to reexamine all our marketing efforts. We need to make

A high-quality experience and the highest-quality food.

certain that every element of our advertising and promotional campaigns as well as the in-store environment at every location reinforce our brand awareness and brand value among our customers. Also, I want Joan to set up a team of her store-management people to see how we can design into our current store layouts shelving for pickup orders, so that customers who ordered online can get their food quickly and avoid any in-store lines. We can call it something like Burger Bistro on the Go.

"We want every customer to feel confident that he or she will receive a high-quality experience *and* the highest-quality food every time they walk into a Burger Bistro.

Changes to our internal process are essential.

"Finally, everyone here knows that our Burger Bistro Way philosophy emphasizes how important it is that we have the full commitment to our shared goals of every team member, including those working the counters and in the kitchens at all ninety-three Bistros. So I want to have a town meeting using our in-house video network to speak with everyone in the Bistros and here at the headquarters. I want to tell them about the challenges we are facing and the new initiatives that we will take to continue to grow as a company; basically, the work that Eileen, Don, Gabe, and Joan will be spearheading for us. And then I'd want to take their questions and hear their ideas and concerns as we move forward.

"I'm familiar with all this," Saul adds, "but it might be better if I have some talking points in front of me for the video town hall. I don't want to sound like some politician who's just winging it." Everyone chuckles at that remark—and then Saul turns to you, sitting along the wall.

"I'll tell you what," he says. "You've been here for a year or so, but you probably have a fresh set of eyes on all this information. Plus, you did your two weeks of counter and kitchen work quite recently, so you may have a better feel for the folks working in the Bistros. Why don't you write a draft for my prepared remarks and then share it with Eileen, Don, Gabe, and Joan?

"You've been sitting here listening," he continues, still speaking to you, "so you have a sense of what I want. Start with a summary of the challenges facing us, but don't make it downbeat. Take a positive tone. Outline the key initiatives that we will be highlighting as we move forward. Don't forget to include all the things we will be doing. Everybody will certainly see the promotional stuff, but the changes in our internal processes are just as essential.

"Remember: I want it to be optimistic and confident. That's how I feel, and that's what I want to communicate to everyone at Burger Bistro! Make it a series of bullets with well-developed sentences that detail the key points everyone needs to know. You think you can do this?"

Optimistic and confident—that's what I want to communicate.

You reply in the affirmative, and Saul ends the session while everyone is still looking at you. "Great!" he says. "Circulate your finished draft to Eileen, Don, Gabe, and Joan by the end of the week."

11

A DOLLAR SAVED, A DOLLAR EARNED

Offering Today's Suppliers a Chance to Become Tomorrow's Partners

"You're still working in a dollar store? Four years of college, and that's the best you can do?"

"Dad, I told you already, I'm not working *in* a dollar store, I work *for* a dollar-store company. I'm on the Dollar Deals Inc. finance team." You've had the job for nearly two years, but your dad still likes to kid you about Dollar Deals. He knows what you do, but his joke has yet to grow old. You're just hoping to wait it out.

Dollar Deals is actually an interesting business and a good place to work. Twenty-eight years ago, its founder and CEO, Alex Gutierrez, shrewdly adopted the business model used by the large national dollar-store chains and has managed to expand the business to include stores in Southern California, Arizona, and Nevada. His strategy combines close attention to every aspect of the business and the discipline to stay out of places where the big dollar-store chains already are. Today there are forty-seven Dollar Deals stores in towns like Barstow, Victorville, Hemet, Blythe, Bullhead City, and Kingman.

Dollar Deals, like other dollar stores, is a little-box store as opposed to the big-box stores like Walmart and Costco. It sells an assortment of household goods, packaged food products, beauty and personal-care products, and over-the-counter medicines. The stores have a no-frills retail environment with a stripped-down design, metal shelves, and a limited selection of products. Each store carries eight thousand to ten thousand items, which is far less than the big-box competitors. But the everyday low prices are usually better than the competition. It's been a winning formula. In the last quarter, same-store sales (sales in existing stores compared to the same quarter in the previous year) increased 3.5 percent on average.

The commute to the head office in San Bernardino isn't ideal, but so far, the job has been worth the driving hassle. Your boss, CFO Dave Lopez, has been with the company almost from the beginning. He's a smart, innovative manager—exactly the kind of boss you can learn from. And that's precisely what you've been doing. You're still not sure whether you'll stay at Dollar Deals over the long haul; certainly not twenty years like Dave. But for now, it's all upside as you continue to learn.

Think of it as "dollar deals" for the company itself.

For the past few months, Dave has had you working with other finance staffers on a special project analyzing Dollar Deals supplier spending in coordination with Ben Gaston, the VP for procurement and supply chain management. You pulled the annual spending data for each supplier, and then Ben and his team assigned an A, B, or C grade based on overall performance, payment terms, on-time delivery, and a number of other measures. What emerged was a towering pile of spreadsheets for nearly every product category in the stores, including paper and plastic goods; kitchen and cookware; small appliances; cleaning supplies; health and beauty aids; basic apparel; home decor; rugs; lamps; coffee; canned goods; frozen foods; and snacks.

"All things being equal, about 80 percent of the cost of purchased goods is probably going to 20 percent of our suppliers, with the rest of the dollars inefficiently spread around the entire supply base," Dave has said. "We need to make sure that every dollar is well spent. Think of it as 'dollar deals' for the company itself." Along with Ben, Dave is intent on developing a new procurement profile that will improve the performance of every supplier while also achieving cost reductions for Dollar Deals. The new profile involves selecting one or two preferred-partner suppliers in each product category who will be on the receiving end of the bulk of Dollar Deals' business while at the same time transitioning out the low-performing suppliers.

A win-win-win—for them, for customers, and for us.

It's been fascinating to see the entire company examined from this perspective—a true learning experience that already has you thinking about how you could manage your next career move, whether with Dollar Deals or elsewhere.

This morning, Dave and Ben have assembled the entire procurement profile team in a conference room at a nearby San Bernardino hotel to review the full-up analysis with Alex and Rita Gelb, VP for store management and merchandising. They're also presenting a one-year transition plan with a timeline showing when the current supplier lineup will be rationalized to eliminate C-level suppliers and move toward negotiating new contracts with preferred-partner suppliers.

One component of the transition plan calls for a supplier summit to which all current suppliers and a selection of prospective new suppliers will be invited. At that meeting, the preferred-partner program will be explained. Suppliers will have the opportunity to meet one-on-one with the appropriate buyers on Ben Gaston's team to discuss their relationship with Dollar Deals and how it will evolve over the coming year.

"I like the approach you guys have outlined here," Alex says, "including the supplier summit. Rita, before I forget, I want you to make a presentation at the summit emphasizing Dollar Deals' promise to provide our customers with quality merchandise at everyday low prices.

They'll be real partners.

"The suppliers need to understand their role in making good on that commitment. Obviously, they want to make a profit, too, but those who are flexible and willing to work with us will be profitable. At the same time, as Dave and Ben's plan makes clear, Dollar Deals will see cost reductions and continue to make good on our commitment to our customers.

"Some suppliers might see this as skimming their profits, but we need to portray the entire effort as a win-win-win—for them, for our customers, and for us. The smart suppliers will work with us as we make this change. Those who remain after the transition will have a tighter relationship with Dollar Deals. They'll be *real* partners. And they're likely to see more revenue too.

"One other thought: while it's not the most important thing, with all the information and the one-on-ones, it looks like the summit will be an all-day event. We should plan for a buffet lunch and maybe a reception afterward for those who want to stick around for a while after the formal meeting ends. It will also give me a chance to meet and talk with some of our major suppliers."

He then turns to look out at everyone in the room. "And finally, I want to thank everyone here who worked on the new procurement profile and the go-forward plan. You guys did a good job. Now the challenge is going to be *implementing* the plan. Supply transitions can be risky and complications can pop up anywhere along the way. I want to have biweekly meetings with Dave and Ben and some of their key people to make sure we're on track every step of the way. And thanks to all of you. I appreciate your work, and I know we can do this."

After Alex leaves, Dave takes over the meeting and, along with Ben, starts planning the next steps and making assignments. As a junior staffer in finance, you expect to be assigned to the team aggregating the total spend for *Underscore his determination to make this a success.* each category and calculating the preliminary estimates of the cost-reduction targets once the preferred partners are selected. That's how it plays out—but then, right out of the blue, Dave adds something else to your assignment.

"Look," he says, "we have some time before the supplier summit. I want you to draft a letter from Alex to all the suppliers inviting them to this event. Have it underscore his determination to make this new approach a success. Make it professional but friendly. And use your judgment about including other information that he needs to cover with the suppliers. As I said, we have some time, but to my knowledge, Alex has never written to the suppliers. So let's make it a home run."

As you drive back to the office you're already focused on Alex's letter. Obviously, it can't include the specifics that led to the A, B, and C ratings, but should it mention that there will be cost-reduction targets for each product category? Is that too much detail? And how about the preferred-partner program? It's going to be highlighted at the summit, but how can you frame it in Alex's letter without having it come across as a threat to some suppliers? Professional but friendly: is that possible? This letter will be trickier than it seems.

12

GOOD NEWS AND MORE WORK AHEAD

Celebrating a Positive Development and Spurring Greater Effort across the Business

You were excited to land your first job out of school last year in the western regional human resources department at AutoUniverse, a major Southern California automotive dealership organization. *What could be more California than its car culture?* you had asked yourself. AutoUniverse owns and operates more than thirty car dealerships across the state and many more nationwide. The dealerships offer a variety of car brands, including eleven dealerships with major US domestic automakers.

For years, US car brands have not sold well in the California market, where consumers have shown a distinct preference for imports. But recently that has started to change. US domestic carmakers' new small and midsize models are starting to attract more attention and more buyers, even in California.

The shift was reported in a recent story that appeared in *AutoTrax*, a leading automotive magazine. The story found that domestic carmakers were starting to gain ground on their imported competitors among California consumers. It detailed some of the changing customer attitudes, especially for small SUV and crossover models. The *AutoTrax* article even said that some owners of the most popular Japanese electric car have been favorably impressed by the Detroit models.

Hal Kettering, VP and general manager of AutoUniverse's western region, read the article this morning and immediately thought that every employee in the domestic dealerships should hear the good news. But, at the same time, he wanted to underscore the need for everyone to stay focused. Crossover SUVs might be among the most successful vehicles in decades for US domestic carmakers, as the article stated, but the leading Japanese company's retail market share in California was still nearly 20 percent, more than any of the US brands. The most significant market share for any domestic brand sold by AutoUniverse was only 9.5 percent. Although that 9.5 percent share was a substantial increase from just 6 percent a few years before, there was still plenty of hard work ahead even with the good news.

Celebrate, but encourage them to keep at it.

Kettering walked into Tom Edsel's office with the *AutoTrax* story in his hand and a smile on his face. Edsel, the HR vice president for AutoUniverse in the western region, is your boss. "Tom," Kettering said, "I want to send a letter to *everyone* working in our domestic dealerships— the local managers, the salespeople, the finance and back-office staffers, the guys on the service counters, the mechanics, everyone. I want them to celebrate what we're accomplishing this year, but I also want to encourage them to *keep at it*. We need everyone to stay focused and to take advantage of our momentum. Let's try to get their competitive juices flowing! I know that writing isn't your strong suit, Tom, but have one of your people draft something and get it to me in the next day or two."

Let's get their competitive juices flowing!

As soon as Hal left his office, Tom walked over to your desk and asked you to draft the letter for Kettering's signature. Like Tom, you've never seen yourself as a writer, but as a new employee, you are hardly in a position to refuse, even though the letter will be signed by the GM, a person you've only met a few times.

After cheerfully accepting the assignment, you quickly get online to find the *AutoTrax* story and read it carefully. The article describes the hard reality that imports conquered the California car market decades ago, but adds that Detroit has reenergized its challenge to the status quo. It quotes several recent car buyers who say how impressed they are with features like the electronic parking assist available on top-of-the-line crossover models. Other consumers cited in the story mention styling and fuel-efficient engines. The article also notes that US manufacturers have significantly increased their advertising expenditures in the California market. "It's a whole new ball game on the West Coast," one competitor says.

You then start to think through the message points that Hal Kettering wants to deliver. Tom said that Hal wants everyone in the domestic-vehicle dealerships to celebrate their shared

It's a whole new ball game on the West Coast.

success, but at the same time, he needs them to stay focused. It almost seems like he wants to inspire them to higher levels of achievement. You've only had one meeting with Hal Kettering—to be totally honest about it, you were simply introduced to him and shook his hand—but Tom has described him as a really informal kind of guy. So his letter shouldn't sound like a pompous pronouncement from someone in a remote corner office. You know instinctively that wouldn't work anyway, since the letter is intended for all sorts of employees, from sales types to mechanics in the service departments.

Getting the right tone is likely to be challenging.

Getting the right tone is likely to be a challenging part of the assignment. The letter also has to be clearly understood by everyone in the company, not just businesspeople. And it has to strike the right balance between celebrating the progress that's been made and presenting the work that remains ahead. It's all doable, but it's not something you're going to throw together easily.

As a new member of the team, you certainly realize that writing this letter is the most high-profile task you've been given so far. It's a task that can establish you as an up-and-coming member of Tom Edsel's HR team, and it might also favorably impress the general manager. But there's no time for daydreaming. Tom wants to see your letter tomorrow. You need to pull together an outline and start writing.

13

UNLIMITED CHALLENGES

Alerting the Board of Directors to the Company's Response to a New Competitive Threat

"It just wouldn't feel like grocery retailing if we weren't faced with a competitive threat every time we turned around," Luis Lozano says. "It's the nature of the business."

"That's true enough, but we should just get on with it," Maria Alondra replies.

In the three years since you joined WFG Inc., you've always known Maria, the company's CFO, to be a direct, no-nonsense, take-charge business executive. Today is no exception. She is sitting in the conference room at the corporate headquarters in Long Beach along with Luis, VP of store operations, and Ed Jenkinson, VP of supply chain and sourcing. You are there with several other staffers brought along to assist the executives with the assignment they received a day earlier from WFG's chairman and CEO, Frank Broadman.

WFG Inc. started in the 1930s as Western Family Grocers. Over the years, it has grown into a major regional supermarket company with 106 stores in California, Arizona, Nevada, Oregon, and Washington. It has nearly thirty-five thousand employees and sales of $11 billion last year. The signage on its stores prominently reads "Family Grocers." The name is intended to foster a sense of kinship with customers.

"Just to get everyone up to speed," Maria continues, "Frank has asked Luis, Ed, and me to put together a team to draft a plan responding to the growing strength of limited-assortment grocery stores. They have expanded quickly back east, and it's only a matter of time before they start to make their presence felt in our regional markets. Frank wants WFG to get ahead of the curve and make changes now that will put us in the best possible position to meet this new competition.

"He wants to present the plan to the board of directors at its next quarterly meeting. That means we have two months to build out a comprehensive and detailed program. This is now the top priority for everyone here," she says as she scans the room.

The supermarket industry has been intensely competitive for as long as anyone can remember. The big-box retailers started moving into groceries in the 1980s along with the warehouse stores and clubs. High-end and organic grocery chains have carved out a place for themselves in the market. Webvan, a pioneering online grocer, went bankrupt in 2001, but the idea of online grocery sales is again showing signs of life. Meal-kit delivery services also are attempting to encroach on the grocery market space. But the fastest growing new entrants to the market are the limited-assortment grocery stores.

Led by several European companies, the limited-assortment category has grown to include well over two thousand stores in the United States. The stores are typically half the size of a traditional

Frank wants to get ahead of the curve.

40,000- to 50,000-square-foot supermarket. More than 90 percent of the products are store brands. As the term *limited-assortment* implies, the selection is usually about three-quarters of what's available at a supermarket. For example, they will stock only one type and one size of ketchup or mustard. They offer less fresh produce as well. In return, the limited-assortment stores deliver average customer savings of about 40 percent, which makes them tough competitors.

"There's not going to be a single, simple way to respond to the limited assortment challenge," Maria says. "We're going to have to take a range of actions that can deliver customer value."

"Well, for starters, I think we need to revisit our approach to private-label products," Ed says. "Right now, we offer about forty thousand products in each of our stores, but far too few of them are WFG private label, with better pricing and good margins. I want to start meeting with our suppliers as soon as possible to ramp up our private-label offerings. My guys have estimated that we can have another twenty-five hundred to three thousand new private-label products on our shelves within a year if we start working at it now."

"That would really help keep customers and attract new ones too," Luis adds. "Another initiative we need to consider is reduced pricing on staples like bread and milk. It's a good way to increase traffic in a supermarket, and as studies always find, customers rarely leave with just the bread and milk."

"It's a workable idea," Maria says, "but I need to get my finance team to analyze the trade-offs incurred with lower prices for staples and estimate the effect on our revenues. We need to look at it more closely, but it's worth pursuing at this point. In fact, when you consider that we carry forty thousand products in our stores, we should look at all our pricing to see how we can strategically offer lower prices on a variety of goods that will keep our customers loyal."

"Now that you've brought up cost analysis, Maria," says Luis, "there are a couple of other ideas that I believe we should consider that could drive revenues and keep customers coming into our stores. But they need to be put through a comprehensive financial review."

He continues, "I'd like to see us expand our assortment of fresh food, deli items, fresh baked goods, and fresh flowers. The limited assortment-stores are still reluctant to do much in these areas. Plus, they don't have the infrastructure that WFG has to support an expansion in these categories. Granted, it would be a considerable investment for us, but it would build off the strengths and the experience we already have."

You have worked for Luis in store management for three years now, and you've come to appreciate the way he combines an easygoing, relaxed

We can call them Family Grocers Limited.

manner with a very incisive and well-considered understanding of the supermarket industry and WFG. Discounting his views on the grocery business would be foolish. Nor is he done speaking.

"The other major initiative we need to plan for is a wholesale conversion of some of our stores in response to the limited-assortment competitors," he says. "Of our hundred-plus stores, a number of them serve urban communities made up of younger professionals without families. Those customers are more likely to forego the extensive offerings of a traditional supermarket for the convenience of a smaller, more limited-choice grocery store. At the other end of the spectrum, we have stores in communities made up of families who are very price-sensitive. They would be attracted to a store that had fewer products and a smaller selection but prices that fit their budget. Entirely different motives in each case, but the same potential interest in a limited-assortment grocery store.

"We need to see how we could selectively convert some of our stores to our own version of limited-assortment. We can even call them *Family Grocers Limited* stores and take the challenge right to the competition. And I propose that we consider hiring someone away from one of the major limited-assortment companies to lead this initiative."

Make it informational, not definitive.

"These are terrific ideas," Maria says. "Obviously, we need to work through each of them to see how they can be implemented and the financial impact of every idea that's been surfaced here. The best way to go about this is to have several project teams, each focused on a separate recommendation: private-label expansion, pricing of staples, an across-the-board pricing strategy, building on our strengths, and restructuring some of our stores. They all need to be reviewed in depth.

"As I mentioned, Frank wants to present a full-up plan at the next board meeting, but his usual approach with something like this would be to send every board member a heads-up memo in advance of the meeting. The idea would be to give them a sense of the direction that he's headed." She then looks down the length of the conference table at you and asks that you draft the memo from Frank to his board members.

"I know that you work for Luis," she says, "but we're all on the same team here. Start with a quick overview of the competitive forces that shaped the

Paint a picture of a winning strategy.

contours of today's grocery industry. The board may not be as familiar with this as we are. Then do a brief summation of each of the key ideas we've identified at this meeting. Keep in mind that there's still plenty of work to be done before our plans are finalized, so you need to make it informational and not definitive. Also, don't simply list the ideas the way they tumbled out on the table here. Put them in the context of our changing market environment and in an order that paints a clear picture of a winning competitive strategy. The message is that WFG is up for this challenge!

"When you're done, send your draft to Luis, Ed, and me. We will share it with Frank early next week when we present him with our next steps and timeline for completing a detailed plan that will be ready for the board to review in two months.

"Thanks, everyone. All of you will hear from us later today with your team assignments. Now the hard work begins."

14

HERE COMES THE FUTURE

Telling the Industry the Company's Story and Vision for the Future

The vibe at FreshFace Essentials Inc. was exactly what you were looking for when you took the job two years ago managing the company's social media and influencer marketing. It's a small, agile, and innovative business that's carving out a place for itself in a fast-changing industry. Your first job after college with an advertising agency always seemed too corporate, with its emphasis on hierarchy. Plus, moving from one client project to the next left you feeling less than fully invested in a specific product category or industry. You were ready to leave after three years.

FreshFace was a two-year-old start-up when you hired on. The founder, Chantel Beaumont, worked in the New York fashion world for years but moved to Los Angeles to launch her skin-care business. With her poise, understated but fashionable style, and distinctive name, Chantel is often thought to be European, but she was raised in a small town in Oregon far from the glamorous continental capitals. She identified skin care as one of the most dynamic categories in the beauty industry, and over the past four years, she's made

The beauty industry is experiencing sweeping changes.

FreshFace an exciting, high-profile brand in a crowded and intensely competitive market.

The beauty industry is experiencing sweeping changes across the board. The big beauty companies that have long dominated the business and sell their luxury brands at huge margins are under assault. The same pressures are being felt by the department stores and large beauty-supply chain stores that distribute their products. Customers are migrating to new start-up brands sold through drugstores, supermarkets, and most significantly online. Today, these mass-market channels account for about 70 percent of beauty sales.

Adding to the pressures reshaping the market are evolving customer preferences. The demand has slowed for heavy cosmetics that offer a smooth, flawless look, while other beauty categories are continuing to grow. For example, products that deliver immediate improvement to under-eye bags and facial lines are becoming increasingly popular with the growing population of older customers. Another category attracting considerable interest is personalized beauty care that combines customer-provided information with artificial intelligence to identify the appropriate skin-care products among the vast number available on databases.

But the skin-care category in general—including creams, lotions, moisturizers, soaps, and scrubs—is experiencing the fastest growth rates. That's especially true of products that offer a connection between beauty, skin care, and clean, natural formulations. FreshFace is right in that sweet spot.

This is a high-profile event. All the large beauty companies attend the expo.

This morning, Chantel has gathered the FreshFace marketing team together in the conference room to discuss an upcoming opportunity to promote the company and its strategic vision. It's a youngish group of the company's marketing leads that she playfully calls her beauty and brain trust. She relies on the team to offer new ideas and to act as a sounding board for her views on how to build the brand. It's an example of the wide-ranging involvement in the business that had attracted you to FreshFace.

Today's meeting has a specific objective. "I've been invited to speak on a panel at the Global Beauty Expo next spring in Las Vegas," Chantel says. "The theme is pretty wide-ranging: 'Ready or Not: Here Comes the Future of Beauty.' This is a high-profile event. All the large beauty companies attend the expo along with quite a few prominent independent companies and start-ups. Industry analysts who follow the business also attend the expo, along with investors looking to make a bet on the newest trends and the companies best positioned to take advantage of the changes working their way through the beauty business. It's a great opportunity, and we need to make the most of it. In particular, we need to do what we can to attract investors who will help us achieve our long-term goals—or perhaps a partnership with a major beauty company that would give us the financial flexibility to pursue our vision while maintaining our creative independence."

We need to attract investors to help us achieve our goals.

Although Chantel doesn't mention it, another possibility is that a major beauty company would offer to buy FreshFace. The acquisition of independent beauty companies is happening regularly across the industry as the major brands seek to take advantage of the independents' consumer appeal while at the same time reducing the threat they present to the big companies' core business. Chantel has never expressed an interest in selling a company that she's nurtured and grown over the past four years. Nor are you sure how it might impact you personally. For the moment, it's not a concern.

"I'd like everyone's help identifying the parts of the FreshFace story that I should highlight in my remarks at the start of the panel discussion," Chantel continues. "Let's use the whiteboard to gather everyone's ideas. Who wants to start?"

"I think we need to underscore our growth in the skin-care category and where it's coming from," says marketing director Janet Hartwell, taking a marker and writing that on the board. "We sell our product through drugstore and beauty-supply channels, but we also move a lot of product through internet sales. The big beauty companies may find that uncomfortable, but it is a fact, and it will continue to be an even larger share of the overall market in the future." Janet is your boss and has been with FreshFace from the start. She has a good perspective on the company's growth and success.

"True enough," Chantel replies, "but we need to do more than just emphasize our growth. Obviously, that's important, but we need make a larger point too. We should play up the fact that we're committed to being a beauty business that strives to be *authentic* and that we have a *passion* for skin-care beauty. Put those two words on the board, Janet."

"Well, to link Janet's point with yours, Chantel," you break in, "we should include something about our social media and internet strategies, since they drive that online revenue for us and every other independent beauty company, and they'll continue to do so for the foreseeable future. FreshFace has 180,000 Instagram followers, double what we had last year." You write the number on the whiteboard. "That's a lot of potential influencers. Teens in particular use social media to select which beauty and skin-care products they should buy. I also need to get an exact count on the number of times the videos on skin care and wellness on our website are viewed. It's in the tens of thousands. I think consumers recognize the strong link between our products and wellness."

You realize that there are a number of separate points in what you just said, but it's a brainstorming session, and they all need to be surfaced, even if they aren't necessarily in any particular order.

"We should mention our pledge to cruelty-free testing of all our products," adds retail marketing manager Kathy Molina as she jots *cruelty-free* on the whiteboard. "That really does matter to millennials and to teens."

"That's right, Kathy," says Molly Rosen, the product development manager. "Social awareness helps define FreshFace. We should also mention that the raw materials for many of our products are imported from West African businesses that are operated by women and employ women. That includes the baobab oil, shea butter, sesame oil, and black soap that we buy from women co-ops in Senegal and Ghana, and the marula oil from Mozambique. Plus, I think this all ties in with the idea of authenticity that Chantel mentioned earlier. We are the real thing!"

"OK, this is a good start," Chantel says, "but we need to prioritize what we have in terms of our business profile and our perspective on the future of skin care. That includes everything up on that whiteboard along with our overall understanding of where the industry is going, including the expanding mass market for all beauty products.

Frame our message in the context of the trends reshaping the industry.

"Another trend I'd want to touch on is the use of AI tools to identify personalized skin-care solutions for individual customers. Somebody please put that on the whiteboard. We're not doing AI at the moment, but I can see how it might really support online sales. It would require a substantial investment of time and money. That's certainly one objective for speaking on this expo panel. If we make it clear that we're a company with a proven track record and the determination to move ahead in the skin-care category—that we have the passion to succeed—it might attract investors that would support our growth. That's a tall order for one panel discussion at the expo, but it's a great place to start the process, and we have time to work on it."

Then Chantel turns to you and asks you to write a clearly organized and detailed first draft of her talking points for the expo panel that highlights the key aspects of the FreshFace story that should be profiled in a panel setting like this. "We have to treat this panel as more than an advertising opportunity, so try to frame our message in the context of the larger trends that we believe are reshaping the industry. Circulate it to the rest of my beauty and brain trust, and then after everyone's had the chance to digest it, we'll meet again to plan our next steps."

15

STAYING IN THE GAME

Balancing the Need for a Costly New Investment with the Promise of Greater Efficiency and Future Growth

Y ou knew it was a demanding job when you accepted the offer, but after several years of auditing assignments with a Big Four accounting firm, you were familiar with long hours and exacting work. The difference here in the Sports Affiliates Inc. controller's department is that you are immersed in many of the company's initiatives, not just its accounting practices. You're getting to see how business is done and the complexity of the challenges the company is facing. The job is an education.

Sports Affiliates started as the Sports Champs chain of sporting-goods stores, with four hundred retail outlets and two distribution centers across the United States. A little more than two years ago, Sports Champs, under the leadership of its dynamic new CEO, Scott Samuels, merged with All-Star Sports, another chain that operates nearly three hundred and fifty stores nationwide. The merged companies took the name Sports Affiliates Inc. for their corporate organization but continue to operate stores under the two brand names that have well-established recognition among customers.

About a year ago, Sports Affiliates acquired Western Camping Supplies Inc., a regional chain focused on outdoor recreation with 103 stores in the western and Rocky Mountain states. The Western Camping Supplies brand name has been retained as well.

The growing competitive pressure in the sporting-goods sector was a major factor in the mergers. Companies like Sports Affiliates are expanding their market presence, eliminating costs, and increasing their purchasing leverage with suppliers in response to the threat from big-box stores and the even more intense competition from online retailers.

There was surprisingly little market coverage overlap between the Sports Champs and All-Star Sports stores, so only a few had been closed to eliminate unneeded operating costs. Western Camping, with its more specific product offerings, only closed a few underperforming stores. In total, Sports Affiliates now operates nearly eight hundred and forty stores.

My IT team will need the understanding and support of the entire company.

But the company remains intent on finding other efficiencies from the mergers. Today's meeting has been called by the CFO, Charlie Swenson, who is leading the corporate drive for increased cost savings, in conjunction with the CIO, Robbie Hernandez. Your boss, Beth Harmon, the controller, is among those in attendance, and each of the three executives has brought along other staff members who will work on the project. Beth brought you.

"OK," Charlie says, "I want to turn this meeting over to Robbie, since he's going to be front and center in leading this project and we want everyone to understand what he is planning. It's an IT initiative, but we all have to stay in the game. Right, Robbie?"

"That's right, Charlie," Robbie replies. "We're looking at a fundamental reworking of the company's information technology systems to improve our overall efficiency and eliminate the costly redundancy of having different legacy IT systems from the three companies that came together in Sports Affiliates. As things stand now, we have multiple people doing similar tasks using different systems. We know how we got here, but it's really important that we move ahead as one company with one system. I wanted to have this meeting to emphasize that my IT team will need the understanding and support of the entire company to make this overhaul a success."

"We got it, Robbie," Charlie says. "I'm sure everyone is willing to help—but explain what you're going to do and how it will add value."

"Well," Robbie begins, "the objective is quite simple. We want to reduce duplication and centralize our business operations in ways that will benefit all three of our store brands. That involves a common IT platform using new enterprise resource planning software for a range of activities including sourcing, inventory management, distribution, and sales. This new ERP software will streamline all our processes across the entire company and make us a more nimble and efficient organization. Essentially, it will provide real-time, accurate inventory and sales data across all of Sports Affiliates.

We want to reduce duplication and centralize our business operations.

"For example, it will be able to take point-of-sales information entered by our sales associates in the stores into a common back office. That will give us the ability to do real-time inventory checks, to manage efficient company-wide purchasing, to offer reliable in-store pickup of products purchased online, and to allow our sales associates to reserve a product for customers. And from the company's standpoint, it will facilitate activities like auditing, calculating margins, and taxes. That will give us more timely and accurate information on the performance of every store and our entire product offering. In short, it'll touch every part of the business."

The new ERP software will streamline our processes and make us more nimble and efficient.

"How is that different from what we have now?" Beth asks.

"It's totally different in scope and reach," Robbie explains. "As I mentioned, right now we have three systems: Sports Champs, All-Star, and Western Camping. Each built its own software over time, and to make matters more complicated, those systems report the information on each product separately. The new ERP software will create one multibrand system for the entire company and eliminate the different brand silos."

"Is this the point where you're going to tell us how much all this is going to cost?" Charlie asks.

Robbie is ready for the question, and he goes straight to the heart of the matter. "We're looking at a charge of $35 million next year to start implementing the new system, and another $35 to $40 million in the following year," he says. "With over eight hundred stores, it's going to be quite an undertaking, but we're up to the task. In fact, I don't think we have a choice. If Sports Affiliates is going to compete in this market in the years ahead, we will need this IT infrastructure to ensure our success. I've got the detailed breakout of the capital expenditure requirements in this report that I want to share with everyone. We should review it now."

"I understand what you're saying, Robbie," Charlie interjects in a woeful tone of voice, "but merging our three brands was in part intended to reduce our cost structure, not require an additional $70 to $75 million in IT spending." He started flipping through the report's pages. "Does this report include estimates of how long it'll be before we start seeing a return on the investment?"

"We should start to see some savings from the new system by the end of the first year," Robbie says, "but building a new ERP system is a long-term investment, and it could be six or seven years before we start to see a significant payback on the expenditure."

It couldn't have been what Charlie wanted to hear, but he reveals little of that in his response. "Well," he says, "let's go through Robbie's plan to see what it is we'll be buying and how we might be able to stretch out the implementation, say over three or three-and-a-half years, so that we can start seeing some benefits while reducing the annual capital expense requirements."

The meeting continues for well over an hour, with Charlie and Beth poring over the implementation and expense analysis that Robbie has provided. They question every detail of the plan, looking for ways to balance the advantages of creating a new ERP system with the cost of the program.

"OK," Charlie says finally. "Let's stop here for now. Robbie, I think we're all in general agreement that we need to have a new ERP, but we need to build it out in phases over at least three years, not two. Look at it this way: we all know that getting a new ERP system up and running is never easy. The process is fraught with unforeseen complexities and issues. Your guys are good, but this extra twelve months will give them additional time to get things right.

"I'd like you to rework your report with support from Beth and her team. When it's ready, the three of us will present it to the boss and see how Scott wants to proceed.

"I want to give him a comprehensive plan detailing what we need to accomplish, along with a timeline and cost analysis. Now that I'm thinking about it, let's also include a draft letter that Scott could send to the entire organization explaining what a new ERP system can achieve and the value it can deliver. Basically, it should be a letter promoting the new IT system and explaining how it will touch everyone's job and make Sports Affiliates a better, more competitive company. It doesn't have to include any of the cost

It'll make Sports Affiliates a better, more competitive company.

information. That will remain proprietary for now. But if we want their cooperation, everyone needs to understand what we're doing as we move forward.

"You're all going to be involved in preparing the report to Scott, but who wants to take a shot at drafting that letter?"

There is a long moment of silence in the conference room. Then you hear yourself say, "I'll do it."

16

NOT OUT OF THE
WOODS YET

Confronting a Pandemic-
Driven Business Crisis

I t seemed like it turned into a roller coaster to hell. The enthusiasm
you experienced when you took the accounting staff job with City
Girl Boutiques, Inc., five years ago has been tested in ways you never
imagined. Established in 1970, the company's more than two hundred
stores on the West Coast, the Chicago area, Florida, and the Northeast
are go-to destinations for young women looking for trendy, stylish clothes
that can be worn at the office or for a night out. The job's certainly been
a great learning experience in a fast-paced, highly competitive industry.
But not long after you joined, the nationwide decline in foot traffic at
shopping malls—where nearly all of the company's stores are located—
started to show up in a slow but steady erosion in year-over-year sales.
Smart merchandising and pricing strategies offset the declines until the
pandemic struck, but the virus changed everything. The company now
finds itself dragged right up to the edge of bankruptcy.

In March, City Girl closed all of its stores temporarily as a result
of the pandemic, with a predictably devastating effect on revenue and
cash flow. Janice Neuman, the CFO and your boss, has had the finance
team working late hours running the numbers and developing the

options she and the CEO, Richard Van Tassel, used to dramatically cut costs. Richard is a skilled retail merchandising expert, but he's had to lean heavily on Janice's financial expertise in the crisis. The company withheld rent payments to mall operators during the closures, furloughed nearly all the staff in its stores, and cut pay for the handful of people still on the payroll.

Starting in midsummer, City Girl stores began to reopen across the country, and almost all of them are now up and running. But sales and earnings continue to show stomach-churning drops. Sales in the quarter ending September 30 fell 50 percent from the previous year, and the company reported a loss of more than $15 million.

In a bid to avoid bankruptcy, Richard and Janice met with City Girl's major shareholders and lenders and worked out a new financial arrangement. Under the terms of the agreement, the company's impending debt payments have been pushed out another twenty-four months until mid-2024, and its lenders agreed to provide another $18 million. Nearly all the company's lenders—almost 99 precent—have agreed to the new arrangement.

It's a glimmer of hope—a faint glimmer.

It's a glimmer of hope—a faint glimmer.

Now, in an early-morning meeting, Richard and Janice are huddled in her office, going over the most recent sales numbers with a few key staffers, including you.

"I don't think anyone knows where this whole thing is going or when we'll hit bottom," Richard says as he slumps in a chair. "Did you see the Commerce Department's monthly retail sales report this morning? Overall retail sales grew by a grand total of 0.6 percent last month. That's even less than the 0.9 percent the previous month. Maybe this is the bottom, but we're going to stay down here for a long while. People are trying to find a new normal, and it might be slower growth for the foreseeable future."

In fact, while the retail sales report was especially troubling for clothing retailers, some retail categories showed healthy gains from the previous year:

- "nonstore" online retailers, +22 percent
- building materials and garden, +15 percent
- sporting goods and hobbies, +11 percent
- food and drink retailers, +10 percent

But other retailers continued to report significant year-over-year declines:

- electronics and appliances, −2.4 percent
- restaurants and food service, −15.4 percent
- gas stations, −15.4 percent

And at the very bottom of the pile was clothing retailers, down −20.4 percent. That was City Girl's category. The only encouraging number for clothing retailers was monthly sales compared to the previous month. They were up 2.5 percent.

"Our creditors have given us some breathing room," Janice said in an apparent effort to get past the gloomy numbers. "We have our costs well in hand. Now we have to do all we can to generate increased sales."

"True enough," Richard replied. "We can only work on the things under our control. The pandemic, along with the fears and concerns it's created, is not something we can deal with. Yet we do have a firm grip on our overall costs. A significant increase in sales is what we

Our creditors have given us breathing room. We have to do all we can to increase sales.

need right now. Longer term, we have to build a robust online sales capability. I intend to work with our entire team to start planning for that. We may be late to the party, but we can learn from what others have done and do it better. We'll also need to bring in some top-notch online sales and marketing expertise. But this is not something that should be widely shared or openly discussed now," he said, lowering his voice to underscore that last point.

"For now," he continued, "our stores are open again and the merchandise is attractively displayed. I bet many of our customers are ready for a new outfit to lift their spirits during this difficult time. And I really like the 'grand *re*opening' approach we're taking in our promotional stuff and the discount pricing that should get people back in the stores. Our new sales slogan works, too: 'Welcome Back! We Have the Look *and* the Deal for You!'

"The new Family & Friends discount cards offering 25 percent off select regular price, sale, and clearance merchandise were just sent by bulk mail to our database of past customers the other day. We should start to see increased revenue from that program in the coming weeks." Richard was sitting up now, his voice regaining some of its typical enthusiasm. He was back in familiar territory.

> *Our message has to be positive and upbeat.*

"The trick will be our follow-through," he continued. "We don't want sales associates or store managers to look or sound uncertain or pessimistic. They need to project a positive, upbeat attitude. At the end of the day, it all comes down to the merchandise on the racks and the salespeople in the stores. They *are* City Girl."

"That's exactly the case, Richard," Janice agreed. "We're doing what we can on this end. We need to have the team out in those two hundred stores see themselves as a key part of City Girl's recovery plan. We should reach out to them directly with that message."

"That's a great idea," Richard said, picking up on the suggestion. "Everyone in the stores needs to see how vital their role is to City Girl's future. Let's send them a personal email from me tomorrow morning. We can portray it as a heads-up on the Family & Friends promotion but also give them a candid outline of the current situation and how we got here. We can touch on some details about the effect the pandemic has had on the retail sector, including City Girl. And I want to say that I understand how disruptive and hurtful the furlough was for them. No use trying to sugarcoat that. But we are open for business now! It's a grand reopening, with promotional pricing and discounts along with our great merchandise. Our message has to be positive and upbeat!"

> *It all comes down to the merchandise on the racks and the salespeople in the stores. They are City Girl.*

He was on a roll now. "I think we can even touch on the new financial arrangements with our lenders. The fact that nearly 99 percent of them agreed to the new terms and delayed payments on our outstanding debt tells you that they believe in City Girl's future. I know that it was in their financial interest not to force us into bankruptcy and only recover pennies on the dollar in a liquidation, but we don't have to go into that! Let's not speculate about their motives. We are still here!"

He turned to Janice and asked, "Is anyone getting this all down? I'd like you to draft that email today. We can look it over before we leave this afternoon."

Richard was still talking, but you already knew that Janice would have you writing that email as soon as the meeting was over. For reasons you don't quite understand, she's identified you as the writer on the finance team. Anything requiring more than a sentence or two seems to land on your desk to be written or edited. She even has you review the grammar and spelling of the financial statement notes on accounting policies, depreciation, inventory evaluation, and the rest. There's no way you won't be tagged for this assignment.

"But we can't kid people," Richard said as he summed up the conversation. "These are difficult times, and we're facing a serious threat. We aren't out of the woods yet, but we know the way. Let's get on with it."

17

WHAT'S NEXT?

Letting Them Know Where You Want Your Career to Go

After one year with Western Insurance Inc., you had your first full-scale performance review this afternoon, and the feedback was positive. It's not that there isn't a vast pile of things you still need to learn about the insurance industry, but Bill Henshaw, your supervisor and manager of the payments and commissions staff, along with Sarah Symington, the director of operations, were positive and encouraging. You left the session feeling good about their assessment but uncertain how to deal with a large, unexpected question they raised.

"You're a quick learner and making a real contribution," Sarah had said. "Stay with it, and you'll have a fine career at Western. In fact, it's not too early to start considering where you might want to work next in operations. Payments and commissions is a great place to start, but think about it and let us know what you believe could be next for you."

Start considering where you might work next.

"Don't spend too much time on that! I want to keep you in P&C as long as I can," Bill had joked.

From the research you did before taking the job last year, you learned that the so-called "back office" really was a good place to start in the insurance industry. It gave you an opportunity to see all the building blocks that are the foundation of the business. Western's regional headquarters in Irvine, California, is responsible for operations throughout the state as well as in Oregon, Washington, Idaho, Nevada, and Arizona. The company sells a full range of life, auto, property, casualty, health, and commercial insurance products through a network of independent insurance agents.

Your job as an analyst with payments and commissions has given you the opportunity to see the scale and complexity of the company. You work with all the product specialists on the P&C team to calculate commissions paid to the agents based on line of products sold, whether it is a new policy or a renewal, and whether there are any special incentives or bonuses that need to be applied. Everything that P&C does is coordinated with the agency operations department, which is the primary point of contact with the independent agents. At first it all seemed overwhelming, but you soon learned your role. Today's performance review was evidence of your progress.

Top 5 percent in every category.

The review focused on the expectations of an early-career employee such as yourself. It included six categories:

- action-oriented
- results/performance-focused
- customer-focused
- time management
- flexibility/adaptability
- team-oriented

You had ranked in the top 5 percent in every category. The "needs improvement" section of the review noted that you should continue to expand your skill set to include planning, organizing, problem-solving, and strengthening peer relationships. It was all very encouraging. Sarah and Bill made it clear that they wanted to help you build your career at Western.

Expand your planning, problem-solving, and peer-relations skills.

But what about that looming question? Did Sarah really want your feedback on what you might be interested in doing next? You're pretty sure she did, so you have started to think about the other possibilities in the operations group. There are several departments that seem interesting:

- **Agency operations** works with the independent agent network and coordinates with all Sarah's other operations departments. You've already had some experience with agency operations through your work for Bill in P&C. The agency team is also responsible for customer care and works with agents in the field to retain policyholders.

- **Claims processing** is responsible for examining insurance claims to determine whether a claim should be paid, denied, or held for further examination by claims examiners or investigators. The department also ensures that insurance claims match the terms of the outstanding policy.

- **New business processing** works with prospective new policyholders. They collected information that underwriters need to determine coverage terms and premiums for each product. And they work with agents in the field to assist them in explaining the range of deductibles and premiums to prospective customers.

- **Policyholder services** is responsible for ensuring that Western's customer service is top-notch. This department is the point of contact for questions from policyholders and supports all the other operations departments, as well the independent agents. Policyholder services is also involved in premium collection and renewals, and it prepares the information that's needed to resolve any outstanding customer issues.

There's some obvious overlap between the various departments, but you don't want to get back with Sarah and tell her that you'll work anywhere. You've decided to give yourself a week to think it over and then pick the one that has the most appeal. And you believe you should include a second choice, just to show her that you're flexible.

An email follow-up seems to be the best approach, but there are a number of decisions you have to make. First, would it be appropriate to just send the email to Sarah? Or should you send it to Bill too, even though it's essentially your pitch to leave his department? Or can you just copy Bill on the email?

And how can you link your choices to the strong ratings you received in the six categories of the performance review? You're not entirely sure how those other departments work or how relevant your ratings are to the needs of those departments. But you want to weave them into the email. The same goes for the items Sarah suggested you should work to develop: planning, organizing, problem-solving, and peer relationships. Might your email connect those development needs to the departments where you'd like to work?

Link your job choices to your strong performance ratings.

You have a week to think it through, but you don't want it to linger any longer. The email you send needs to show Sarah and Bill that you were listening. Their performance review spelled out your strengths and the things you should focus on to advance your career. You also got an open invitation to help them determine your next position with Western.

Now what are you going to do about it?

APPENDIX

Case Analysis Worksheet

Audience/s:	
Message/s:	

Key Facts	Outline
•	I.
•	II.
	III.
•	IV.
•	V.
	VI.

Case Writing Checklist

Element	Details	Score	
		Student	Instructor
Analysis	Have you delved into the issues in the case or merely summarized the facts?		
Organization	Did you start with an outline and make certain that your writing reflects logical, orderly thinking?		
Diction	Are your word choices exact and appropriate? Have you used phrases and words that are compelling and persuasive?		
Clarity	Have you expressed your ideas and recommendations in a simple, clear, and accessible way?		
Editing	Have you proofread and spellchecked your writing? Have you read it aloud to check for tense agreement, run-on sentences, and fragments? Are the sentences too long or awkward? Is the punctuation correct?		
Conclusion	Do you offer an appropriate summary based on the purpose of the writing assignment (e.g., next steps, timelines, encouragement, a projection of confidence)?		

Scoring Scale

Not Effective   Somewhat Effective   Effective

| 1.0 | 1.5 | 2.0 | 2.5 | 3.0 |

A Quick Reference Guide to Basic Business-Writing Formats

This guide offers a summary of some basic types of business writing. For more detailed information, consult one of the many format guides available in print or online.

Business Letters

Yes, companies still send letters. They are appropriate for communicating with individuals and organizations outside the organization, including customers or suppliers.

Use the Company Letterhead

Date
Name
Title
Company
City, State, Zip

Dear Name:

The **introductory paragraph** states the purpose of the letter in a direct, professional, and friendly way. Be concise and to the point, or you'll risk losing your reader.

The **second paragraph** describes the importance of your message and how it relates to the company or individual to which it was sent.

Subsequent paragraphs provide additional background and other information to support the purpose of your correspondence and make reference to any enclosures. This is where your writing skill really comes into play. Do not go on at great length. Be concise and try to keep it to a single page. If your letter is longer, edit it to make the language tighter. But this is a general rule, depending on complexity; obviously some letters will be longer than one page.

The **closing paragraph** restates the purpose of the letter and, if appropriate, thanks the recipient for an anticipated response. This can be as simple and direct as "I will follow up with you by phone next week" or "I look forward to discussing this matter with you at the upcoming trade show" or "I look forward to your response."

Sincerely,

Your signature

Email and Memos

Most organizations use a simple and direct format for internal email and memos. Some companies, perhaps most famously Procter & Gamble, have a detailed and explicit approach to memo writing.[15] Unless your company has a specific style, use the following:

TO: Name

CC: Name (if any)

FROM: You

SUBJECT: Describe the purpose or objective of the email/memo. If possible, use the Subject line to pull in the reader or to start selling your idea.

DATE: Month day, year

Start with your **key message**, main idea, or recommendation. Be direct and to the point.

- Use highlighting devices (like these bullet points) to **make your important message elements stand out** so that busy people can skim the email and get your point. Email and memos do not qualify as pleasure reading. Everyone gets dozens daily.

- Write **short sentences** and **brief paragraphs;** use only as many words as necessary.

- Use your facts to **build the message logically**.

- **Describe the benefits** and value of your proposal.

- Conclude by outlining your proposed **next steps** or solicit the reader's advice, input, support, and/or permission to move forward.

No signature or name required.

---

[15] Search "P & G Memo" online to see a full explanation of the Procter & Gamble one-page memo structure.

Talking Points

It is a well-known fact that an audience can hear when someone is reading a speech. We have all seen someone struggle through a prepared speech in a stilted monotone and then have an abrupt change in vocal tone and even body language when a Q&A follows the talk. Few of us have an actor's ability to memorize lines of dialogue and own them. In most business situations, it's best not to even try.

Instead, speak informally while using talking points to keep the message on track. Using talking points will help maintain the conversational, audience-focused authenticity that a business presenter should strive to achieve.

Here are a few basics for writing and using talking points. First, include a **brief header** that contains the topic and audience for the talking points. Then, list the talking points, keeping the following in mind:

- Talking points **are not to be read** and they should be **easily scanned**.

- Keep them **short,** but do use complete thoughts. This will assist the presenter if they draw a blank while speaking or might fail to mention an important element of a bulleted point.

- Use **subheads** that organize your talking points into logically ordered groups.

- Start with **goals or objectives**.

- List the **facts or key messages in priority descending order** to make the message compelling and easy to follow.

- If they can help the message, **offer examples**, but keep them brief and on point.

- Wrap up with **a summary bullet** explaining how the recommendations best serve the needs of the organization.

- **Solicit audience buy-in** and enlist their support and advice as things move forward.

Having talking points does not mean that practice isn't needed. Encourage presenters to practice (not just read through the points) so that they are familiar with the material. This might seem like something a presenter would do with a speech, but with talking points, the practice is to **internalize the ideas, not the words.**

US Department of Transportation Bumping Policy[16]

Q: Is the amount an airline must offer involuntarily bumped passengers arriving on a substitute flight within 1–2 hours of the original flight still 200% of the one-way fare, with a maximum of $675, and is that the maximum the DOT requires, or the maximum that the airline will offer (200% of some flights would be way over $675)?
A: Yes, an airline must offer 200% of the one-way fare up to $675 to involuntarily bumped passengers arriving on a substitute flight within one to two hours of the planned arrival time of their original domestic flight. Airlines are to free to offer involuntarily bumped passengers more money than required.

Q: Is the amount an airline must offer involuntarily bumped passengers arriving on a substitute flight over 2 hours after their original flight still 400% of the one-way fare, for a maximum of $1,350?
A: Yes, an airline must offer 400% of the one-way fare up to $1350 to involuntarily bumped passengers arriving on a substitute flight over two hours after the planned arrival time of their original domestic flight. Airlines are free to offer involuntarily bumped passengers more money than required.

Amount of Denied Boarding Compensation—Domestic Transportation

0 to 1 hour arrival delay	No compensation.
1 to 2 hours arrival delay	200% of one-way fare (but no more than $675).
Over 2 hours arrival delay	400% of one-way fare (but no more than $1,350).

Amount of Denied Boarding Compensation—International Transportation

0 to 1 hour arrival delay	No compensation.
1 to 4 hours arrival delay	200% of one-way fare (but no more than $675).
Over 4 hours arrival delay	400% of one-way fare (but no more than $1,350).

---

[16] US Department of Transportation, "Airline Consumers' Rights FAQ," last modified April 18, 2017, https://www.transportation.gov/airconsumer/faq.

ABOUT THE AUTHOR

Dennis Signorovitch is an adjunct professor at Mount Saint Mary's University, Los Angeles, where he teaches management communications in the Department of Business Administration. He also created and sponsors the department's annual Business Writing Challenge for undergraduates. Previously, he worked for nearly thirty years in executive-level communications roles with several major US corporations. During that time, he also served a term as chair of the Aerospace Industries Association's communications council. In 2006, he established Mount Saint Mary's Vantage Point Forum speaker series that brings business leaders to campus to share with students their perspectives on the business world and the challenges and opportunities facing women in business.

Printed in the United States
by Baker & Taylor Publisher Services